WASHINGTON STATE
TROUT FISHING

A Guide to Lakes

WASHINGTON STATE
TROUT FISHING

A Guide to Lakes

Dan Homel

Forrest-Park Publishers
Bellingham, Washington

Forrest-Park Publishers
Post Office Box 29775
Bellingham, Washington
98228-1775

PRINTED IN THE UNITED STATES OF AMERICA

ISBN: 1-879522-03-9

CREDITS

Electronic pre-press and cover mechanicals
prepared by Marcus Yearout.

Photographs: Daniel Homel.

Fly drawings and frontis by Edward Ruckey.

Darkroom work: Quicksilver Photo Lab.

Special Thanks to the following individuals who contributed
to the material or photographs contained herein; either by con-
versation, participation, or inspiration: Mark Hurlbert, Ed and
Bruce Ruckey, Hugh Lewis, Jim Johnston, Randy, Cyrus and
Brandon Gates, Joe and Will Homel, Harold Jellison, Errol
McWhirk, Richard and Diane Van Demark, Ralph Wahl, and
Thomas Cicchitti.

The following groups or institutions were especially cooperative in providing data, information, or assistance in the compila-
tion of this text: The Washington Department of Fish and
Wildlife, The United States Forest Service, The Fourth Corner Fly
Fishers, The Western Washington University Research Library,
and The Bellingham Public Library.

On the cover: Mark Hurlbert displays a rainbow trout caught
at Lake Lenice in the Crab Creek Wildlife Area of Grant County.

TABLE OF CONTENTS

Introduction 9
Preface 11

Trout Species in Washington Lakes
Rainbow Trout 16
Cutthroat Trout 18
Brown Trout 21
Brook Trout 21
Kokanee 22
Miscellaneous Species 23

A Listing of Washington Trout Lakes
Alphabetical by County 27

Fly Fishing
Tackle for Washington Lakes 73
Techniques for Washington Lakes 83
Progressive Techniques for the Non-Fly Fisher 93
Washington Lake Fly Patterns 99

Conservation
Ways to Bring About Positive Change .105

Bibliography 109

INTRODUCTION

Washington State Trout Fishing - a guide to lakes, is a useful reference book for both the experienced and novice angler. Travelers and residents new to the region will find valuable advice and proven methods for successful trout fishing in Washington lakes. Any of these techniques can apply to other areas of the Pacific Northwest as well. Seasoned Washington fishermen will hopefully find some new bits of information here; or be inspired to try a lake they have not fished before.

Fly fishing is emphasized throughout the book, but we have in no way inferred that this is an exclusive or "best" method. In fact, a short section is devoted to techniques for the non-fly fisher or the average parent taking the kids out on opening day. However, with increased opportunities to fish for large trout in some of the "fly-fishing-only" lakes and quality "special regulations" lakes, fly fishing knowledge is certainly recommended. On many waters, at various times of the year, fly fishing can produce results when all other methods fail.

PLEASE BE AWARE OF THE FOLLOWING:

When traveling to, or exploring, a new destination we urge you to call ahead for local information and current road or trail conditions. Also, it is prudent to inquire locally about the status of any boat launch facilities, handicapped access, and campgrounds since these amenities are often subject to adverse weather, low water levels, or deferred maintenance. Of course, caution is always advised when engaged in any outdoor activities, such as those described in this book.

As a final note; remember to check the current state regulations before fishing a particular lake (or tributary stream). This book can provide general information; however, fishing laws change constantly. Only the current state regulations should be relied upon. Free copies of the game fish regulations are available from Washington fishing license dealers.

PREFACE

There are an amazing variety of lake types in Washington State. A number of natural lakes, particularly those in the northern part of the state, were carved out by glaciers during the Pleistocene period. Many more are called "kettle lakes" because they were formed in depressions left by melted glacial deposits. Another common type of natural lake in Washington is the "slide" lake, which came into being when landslides blocked an existing valley or canyon. Still other small ponds or marshes are formed by beaver activity.

Man-made waters also abound. Most are simply the result of a dam being placed on a stream, which impounds it's flow. Several natural lakes have been increased in size by the strategic placement of a dam near the outlet, thus forming a "new" lake. Seep lakes are another form of man-made lake, brought about by seepage from irrigation waters that fill ancient, dry depressions and rocky coulees.

All this adds up to abundant habitat for the species of trout that reside in Washington. Some lakes are suitable for wild, self-reproducing trout, while others need to be supported by heavy pre-season catchable or fry plants. A growing number of these fry planted lakes are being managed as quality waters, which provide bigger trout through special regulations. The objective of this book is to identify a good sampling of each type of lake experience that can be available to the angler. In addition to these lake "listings", we have also included information on the different trout species, recommended fishing tackle, local Washington insect hatches and fly fishing techniques, along with some tips for the non-fly fisher.

Washington State has a rich angling history. Zane Grey, the famous western novelist, fished in the Stilliquamish drainage prior to 1920. A few years later, while still in the logging business, a young writer named Roderick Haig-Brown explored some of the same areas. Haig-Brown, of course, went on the become one of the most respected fishing authors of the 20th century, as well as a Vancouver Island Magistrate.

Beginning about 1930, a quiet gentleman from Whatcom County pursued steelhead, cutthroat, and resident rainbow trout in lakes and rivers throughout the Northwest. His name is Ralph Wahl. Ralph is best known as a pioneer steelhead fly innovator, author and photographer, but has many tales to tell about the early days of casting to trout in lakes. He often mentions fishing trips to various Washington destinations with his friends. Some were fellow members of the Fourth Corner Fly Fishers or the Washington Fly Fishing Club. A companion on quite a few of these early outings was the late Enos Bradner, author of Northwest Angling - a great treatise, now out of print.

I am privileged to know Ralph Wahl, who at 88 years is more able to recall memories than most men half his age. Through our conversations I have learned much about early fishing in this State, the likes of which we may never see again. Perhaps you know someone like this. Someone that gives your fishing a kind of center, a history, a sense of feeling that these lakes, and the fish in them, were passed to you for only a short while. And that you, in turn, must preserve them and the stories they hold, for future generations.

Dan Homel
Bellingham
Whatcom County, Washington

14" native rainbow trout from Ross Lake

TROUT SPECIES
IN
WASHINGTON LAKES

Trout are the most popular fresh water game fish in Washington State. The species of trout that are native to Pacific Northwest waters are the rainbow and cutthroat. Dolly varden are native as well, but are classified as a "charr". Species introduced by stocking programs include brown trout, golden trout, eastern brook and lake trout (both charrs), and grayling. Two species of salmon can be found landlocked in certain Washington lakes; these are the kokanee (freshwater sockeye salmon), and the coho (freshwater silver salmon).

All of the trouts, charrs and salmon are classified as the scientific family *Salmonidae*, which also includes the grayling and whitefish. Salmonids are known as "soft-rayed" in contrast to largemouth bass, bluegill, perch and the like, which are commonly referred to as "spiny-rays". Most anglers have noticed the sharp, hard spines in the dorsal fin of a bass or bluegill, which accounts for the name. Salmonids, on the other hand, lack these spines, possess an adipose fin, and have rather fine scales.

Salmonid survival depends on particular habitat requirements including cool, clean water with a high oxygen content. For natural reproduction, a fine gravel spawning bed, free of silt or debris, is necessary.

Generally, most of the trout, landlocked salmon, and char available to anglers in Washington are stocked. The Washington Department of Fish and Wildlife stocks over 600 lowland lakes and 200 alpine lakes, annually, with both catchable-size and fingerling ("fry") age trout, as well as warmwater fish. Total number of fish stocked yearly for all species is approximately 30 million. In addition to annual stocking programs that provide a put-and-take recreational fishery, the WDFW manages a variety of lakes for wild, self-perpetuating populations of trout. In recent years, additional lakes have been designated as "quality waters" with selective fishery regulations to insure sustaining numbers of larger, more challenging trout. These lakes usually have gear restrictions imposed (no bait or fly fishing only, and barbless hooks) with low limits or catch and release rules.

The State of Washington offers diverse opportunities to all anglers in terms of conditions, water types and species available. One can choose to release trophy rainbows or browns from a desert lake, take home a stringer of catchable rainbows from a lowland pond, or fly fish for cutthroat and brook trout high in the Cascades.

RAINBOW TROUT *(Oncorhynchus mykiss)*

Until 1990 the rainbow trout, in both the sea-run (steelhead) and resident variety, was designated *Salmo gairdneri* in honor of Meredith Gairdner, the Scottish naturalist and physician who collected the first Pacific Northwest rainbow for scientific study. Although it still falls under the large family grouping as a Salmonid, the scientific community felt that the Pacific Coast trout is more closely related to the pacific salmon (genus;

Oncorhynchus) rather than the atlantic salmon (genus; Salmo).

The coastal rainbow trout is native to those waters flowing into the Pacific Ocean from Alaska to Mexico. It has been introduced world-wide, and is still present in most of its natural range.

Rainbow trout, reared in hatcheries, are the main component of the lowland lakes fishery in Washington. Many lakes are stocked, prior to opening day, with thousands of catchable-size trout and large, surplus broodstock. Other lakes receive plants of trout fry, that grow over a years time to catchable-size. Fry plants of rainbow trout in Eastern Washington lowland lakes have been more successful than at comparable waters in Western Washington. The return to the "creel" of planted rainbow fry, west of the Cascades, has averaged less than 20%, as compared to 70% for similar Eastern Washington lakes. Variables that effect western lakes to a greater extent are higher bird predation, higher disease loss, and slower growth due to lower lake productivity. In order to create the best recreational fishing opportunities for license holders, the Washington Department of Fish and Wildlife has developed, through years of study, rainbow trout broodstocks of various strains that serve as progenitors of both catchable and fry stocks. Studies show that different strains of rainbow trout have evolved special traits such as increased thermotolerance, potential longevity, or simply better color. This last point seems a bit shallow, but who wants to catch an ugly trout!

For those anglers who are curious, it may be interesting to know how some of our broodstocks came to be. Two of the rainbow trout broodstocks most commonly used by the WDFW are the South Tacoma and Spokane (named for the hatchery of origin). The South Tacoma rainbow have become one of the primary broodstocks for the catchable, put-and-take fishery in Western Washington. The original eggs are believed to have come from wild rainbows taken from the McCloud River in California. The fish were further developed at the Meador Trout Facility in Idaho, before coming to Washington. The Spokane Rainbow Trout stock was originally taken from the McCloud River and later selected and cultured at the Cape Cod Trout Company in Massachusetts. In 1942 the eggs were shipped to the Spokane Hatchery and then distributed to other facilities in Washington. This strain has been used extensively in the Columbia Basin.

Whether native, wild (self-sustaining) or stocked; rainbow trout in Washington lakes have many common characteristics. The name, "rainbow", is attributed to the prominent red or pink streak running down the side of the fish from just behind the gill cover to the tail. Rainbow sides are olive to green-blue above and silvery below. Small, dark spots of irregular shape and size are scattered on the body. These spots are more evenly distributed on the sides and tail. Rainbow trout can show a great variation in color depending on where they are found, the season of the year, and their genetic strain. The Washington Department of Fish and Wildlife has developed late summer and fall spawning strains, so the fish will reach optimum size at the best planting times of the year.

Rainbow trout thrive in lakes that have an abundance of aquatic insect life. They feed on small invertebrates and insects such as mayflies, damsel flies, caddis flies, and chironomids. Larger rainbows can also be "piscivorous", feeding on other fish.

CUTTHROAT TROUT *(Oncorhynchus clarki)*

Three types of cutthroat trout can be found in Washington; the coastal, the west-slope, and the introduced lahontan cutthroat. Their scientific name is derived from that of Captain William Clark, one of the leaders of the Lewis and Clark Expedition, during which an early catch of the fish was documented.

The coastal cutthroat trout is primarily found in rivers and streams that flow to the Pacific Ocean or Puget Sound. It is usually of the sea-run variety and has a native range from Northern California to Southeast Alaska. The coastal "cutt" is also found

Cutthroat trout taken on soft hackle flies, during the fall, at a Western Washington lowland lake.

in some reservoirs and large still-waters such as Lake Washington and Lake Sammamish. These fish closely emulate their sea-run brethren in the way that they utilize small tributary streams of the lakes to spawn. Resident forms of the coastal cut-throat are also available in small Western Washington beaver ponds.

The west-slope cutthroat trout, often called "native" cutthroat, exists in a range that extends to parts of Montana, Idaho, Wyoming, Western Canada, and Eastern Washington. The vari-ety of west-slope cutthroat that predominates in Washington high lakes is the "Twin Lakes" strain. Old timers may refer to these fish as Montana Black Spots but, in fact, these fish came from broodstock that originated in Washington's Twin Lakes, north of Lake Wenatchee. The west-slope cutthroat does well in clear, cold waters, so the WDFW has used them extensively in its of high altitude lakes aerial stocking program. They have even been planted in lakes once barren of fish life.

The Lahontan cutthroat has been introduced into several east-side Washington lakes, such as Lenore and Grimes. These fish are derived from broodstock originating in the Pyramid Lake area of California. Lahontans can grow in excess of ten pounds and have been successful in highly alkaline lakes where other trout cannot survive.

The cutthroat is often an easy fish to identify due to the orange or red slash mark that is visible under each side of the lower jaw. This slash mark may not be recognizable in juveniles or fresh, sea-run adults. Back and sides can vary from steel-blue to green in color with more consistent, regular shaped spots than the rainbow. The cutthroats tail is slightly forked with a high concentration of spotting. A definitive characteristic that distin-guishes it from the rainbow is the presence of small Hyoid teeth behind the tongue of the cutthroat.

Maturing cutthroat trout generally feed on large invertebrates such as insects or fresh water shrimp. As adults they often sub-sist on small fish fry.

BROWN TROUT *(Salmo trutta)*

Commonly called "german brown", this excellent game fish has been introduced to a growing number of Washington lakes. It was originally imported to the United States from Europe, and has the ability to tolerate water temperatures as high as 75 degrees. In terms of fingerling plants in Washington, it's numbers are small when compared to rainbow or cutthroat trout. Statistics from an example year (1991) indicate that 364,095 browns, 1.4 million cutthroat, and 7 million rainbows were stocked as resident fingerlings. The size of the brown trout fingerlings are bigger, however, and the catchable-size brown trout plants seem to be increasing. A reasonable assumption is that the brown trout will play an important part in the future of Washington fresh water fishing.

Brown trout are distinguished by relatively large, dark spots appearing on the back and sides, together with beautiful red spots, surrounded by pale borders, scattered over the body. The base color of the back is green-brown to olive, while the lower portions of the body are yellow, blending to off-white near the underside.

Small browns consume earthworms, crayfish, and aquatic insects including mayflies and caddis flies (sedge). Mature brown trout feed heavily on smaller fish.

BROOK TROUT *(Salvelinus fontinalis)*

The "brookie" or eastern brook trout, is not native to Washington, but has become well established in small streams, headwater ponds, and in larger lakes having cool, well-oxygenated lower layers of water. This trout's native habitat lies in Eastern North America extending from the Appalachian Mountains to Northern Labrador and Quebec in Canada.

In suitable waters, Washington brook trout can reach a size of 5 pounds, but in many small lakes and streams populations become excessive and growth is stunted due to high competition for food.

Brook trout are, in the opinion of many, the most beautiful of all fresh water game fish. Their coloration varies from dark blue or gray-blue to dark green on the back and sides to white on the belly. The lower portion of the fish may be red to orange. Intricate, worm-shaped tracks called vermiculations occur on the back and upper portions of the body, accompanied by red spots on the sides (often with blue rings about them). The tail is somewhat square and accounts for the old eastern nickname "square tail". The lower fins are tipped white.

Fly fishing is particularly good for brook trout since their diet consists mainly of aquatic insects. Because many small lakes and streams are well-populated with little, eager brookies, they are a good species to pursue for fast, sure action.

KOKANEE *(Oncorhynchus nerka)*

Kokanee are thought to be native to a few landlocked drainages along the Pacific coast. It is actually a variety of sockeye salmon that has been developed for fresh water introduction exclusively. Unlike a majority of sockeye salmon, the kokanee completes it's entire life cycle in fresh water. They can reproduce naturally in some lake environments and die after spawning like a true salmon. Where kokanee have become over-prolific and stunted, the State has established bonus catch limits.

At first glance the kokanee might resemble a trout, but several distinct differences can be easily identified. Foremost, is the deeply forked tail. Another is the proportion of the peduncle (end of the body at the tail), which extends further into the rayed portion of the tail as compared to other Salmonids. A sure identification is found in the number of full-length rays in the anal fin. On trout the rays number no more than 12, and on a kokanee you will observe least 13. The common coloration of the fish is blue on the back with silver sides.

Coho salmon *(Oncorhynchus kisutch)* are stocked in a few Washington lakes, but to a lesser degree than kokanee. These can be distinguished by the body, which is less-elongated, and the sweeping, sickle-shaped anal fin.

Kokanee feed almost exclusively on minute zooplankton and possess an unusual number of fine gill rakers for filtering their diet. Despite the size of their preferred food, kokanee are attracted to flashy lures and flies (I have had kokanee attack gaudy, iridescent flies that were completely passed over by rainbows in the same lake). Kokanee and landlocked coho travel in large schools, so once a group is located, fishing can be fast.

MISCELLANEOUS

Dolly varden are native to Washington and occur in fastwater rivers or at outlets of lakes. They can be anadramous, migrating to saltwater where possible. Unfortunately, at this writing, Washington populations are greatly depleted and closed seasons may be in effect. Please help to protect this fine game fish.

The Grayling has been introduced to Washington lakes in limited numbers. Water must be very cold and pristine. Grayling identification is unmistakable due to the spectacular, high dorsal fin. They spawn in shallow streams and feed on terrestrial as well as aquatic insects. Most grayling caught in Washington are small.

Golden trout have been established in a few remote, high Cascade lakes in Washington. The native habitat of this beautiful fish is the South Fork of the Kern River and it's tributaries in California. It has been introduced by hatchery programs throughout the Western United States. Coloration of golden trout can be dramatic, especially at spawning time when the fins turn a deep orange and the gill covers become red-hued. It can be distinguished from the adult coastal rainbow by virtue of side patterns called parr markings. This environmentally sensitive fish requires stream spawning areas to reproduce a population large enough to withstand moderate fishing pressure. Goldens often interbreed with other trout, forming hybrids, and thus may become eliminated as a distinct species when stocked in waters containing other types of trout.

Lake trout or "mackinaw" are taken in a few deep Washington lakes, where they have the ability to spawn on rocky shelves in 6 to 20 feet of water. For the most part, big lake trout are pursued with heavy trolling tackle and deep-running lures.

Whitefish are primarily found in streams, but have been introduced in a few lakes and have become distributed in the Columbia Basin irrigation system. They are closely related to trout and salmon.

Spiny-rays, although not the main topic of this book, have been known to save an otherwise unsuccessful summer trout fishing trip. Largemouth and smallmouth bass, crappie, bluegill, yellow perch and walleye all fall into this category. Many Washington lakes are developing a strong warmwater fishery, and hardy spiny-rays may provide the main ingredient to a future fresh water sport fishery in urban areas where the habitat and environment are changing. A wonderful account of how the spiny ray fish were introduced to the Pacific Northwest is presented in the classic regional book, The Coming of the Pond Fishes (1946) by Ben Hur Lampman.

Brook trout from a small alpine lake (5,100 ft. elevation) in the North Cascades.

The angler hiking-in to Lenice Lake can expect strong, fry planted rainbow trout.

A LISTING OF WASHINGTON TROUT LAKES

ADAMS COUNTY

Halfmoon Lake - A 26 acre lake with a small, rough boat launch, located 5 miles northwest of Othello off McManamon Road. Trout fingerlings are stocked, but because of poor survival rates, fishing must be evaluated on a year to year basis. A short hike to Morgan Lake, a favorite with fly fishers.

Lyle Lake - Fair fishing for rainbow trout on this 22 acre lake north of Othello. Small boat launch. Try also Herman Lake after parking at Lyle.

Quail Lake - A hike-in fly fishing only lake located in the Columbia National Wildlife Refuge. Check current regulations for catch and release information.

ASOTIN COUNTY

Alpowa Grade Impoundments - Three small ponds off the Snake River (Evans Pond, Golf Course and Silcot Ponds) offer good early season fishing for planted rainbow trout.

Headgate Pond - Stocked well for opening day with rainbow trout, this impoundment off Asotin Creek is open only to juvenile anglers 14 years and younger, and complimentary license holders.

CHELAN COUNTY

Beehive Reservoir - A 12 acre lake approximately 2 miles northwest of Squilchuck State Park providing fair fishing for rainbow and eastern brook trout. Check current regulations for catch and release and selective fishery during later part of season.

Clear Lake - Fair early season fishing for rainbow and eastern brook trout. This small, 5 acre lake is located 6 miles south of the Wenatchee Heights area via the Stemilt Creek Road. Check for selective fishery regulations.

Fish Lake - A 513 acre lake that is usually heavily stocked with rainbow trout. Good fly fishing for rainbows during spring and fall. Some large brown trout also. May be slot limits on trout here, so check regulations.

Lake Chelan - Fishing for kokanee is best April - June on this unique, landlocked fjord. Catchable size rainbow trout are planted during the summer in the lower lake area. Some excellent fishing for wild rainbow trout can be had throughout the upper lake basin above 25 mile creek. Be sure to check the current Department of Fish and Wildlife regulations for numerous tributary stream-mouth closures during the spring. These are to protect pre-spawning adult trout.

Lilly Lake - A 15 acre lake containing rainbow and eastern brook trout, located near Clear Lake. May be catch and release regulations in effect during summer and fall.

Wapato Lake - Located 10 miles northwest of the town of Chelan, this 186 acre lake yields good rainbow trout catches in the early season. Check regs. for catch and release information August -Oct.

Lake Wenatchee - Many small kokanee are caught here, beginning in April. Check for closed season on dolly varden.

CLALLAM COUNTY

Aldwell Lake - A 240 acre lake formed by a dam on the Elwah River. It is located off Highway 101, approximately 6 miles southwest of Port Angeles. Summer fishing is fair to good for wild rainbow trout. Check for selective fishery regulations. The Elwha River upstream from Aldwell Lake to Mills Lake provides one of the few opportunities in Washington to present a fly to native, non-migrating rainbow trout. Special regulations apply here as well.

Beaver Lake - A 44 acre lake containing 6 to10 inch cutthroat. It is located 12 miles south of Clallam Bay via Highway 112 and Burnt Mountain Road.

Crescent Lake - Bearer of the famous Beardslee trout sub-species found only in this lake. These fish are usually caught deep-trolling and can reach 10 pounds or more. A very special-ized fishery that is regulated by the Olympic National Park

Service. Call (206) 452-4501 for information from the Park Service on current conditions of Crescent as well as Ozette Lake also contained within the park.

Pleasant Lake - A large lake near Highway 101 with boat launch and beach containing cutthroat and kokanee. Check current catch and size (slot) limits on kokanee.

Lake Sutherland - A 370 acre lake planted yearly with cutthroat and rainbow trout. The lake is located along Highway 101 about 12 miles west of Port Angeles. Kokanee fishing can be excellent at times.

CLARK COUNTY

Battle Ground Lake - Located within Battle Ground State park, take Heisson Road north from the town of Battle Ground. This 30 acre lake in a volcanic cavity is heavily stocked for opening day with rainbow trout and usually some 20 - 24 inch hatchery rainbow broodstock. Eastern brook trout have been stocked here as well. No internal combustion motors are allowed.

Fargher Lake - This small pond of 3 acres is located north of Battle Ground, off Highway 503. Contains stocked brown trout and can be good in the fall.

Klineline Ponds - Good early season fishing for rainbow and brown trout in these two ponds located next to Salmon Creek, just west of I-5.

Lacamas Lake - Just north of Camas, it contains brown trout. A small Department of Wildlife access exists but caution is urged when launching a boat.

COLUMBIA COUNTY

Beaver, Blue, Deer, Rainbow, Spring and Watson Lakes - Small bank fishing-only lakes strung out along the Tucannon River, north of Camp William T. Wooten State Park. Stocked with rainbow trout. Check regulations for early, short season.

Big Four Lake - Open to fly fishing only, this small lake off the Tucannon Road is often stocked with surplus broodstock rainbow trout. Check regulations for special season and limits.

Curl Lake - A 3 acre lake that is handicap-accessible. Curl is used as a steelhead smolt acclimation pond and does not open until late in the season. It is stocked with rainbow trout in the summer, so fishing is steady until fall.

COWLITZ COUNTY

Castle Lake - Located in the Mount St. Helens National Volcanic monument. A chance for the adventurous angler to fish for large rainbow trout. Requires a long drive on non-maintained logging roads and a difficult hike down a steep hillside to the lake. The WDFW indicates that trout up to 10 pounds have been reported. At the time of this writing there was a selective fishery regulation in effect, with a one fish catch limit and 16 inch minimum size limit.

Coldwater Lake - A large, 700 acre lake formed after the eruption of Mt. St. Helens. It is located off Highway 504 in the Mount St. Helens Volcanic National Monument. The lake contains rainbow trout, stocked as fingerlings in the late 1980's, that have become large, and self-propagating. Cutthroat trout also inhabit the lake, and are believed to be survivors of the eruption. Fishing was excellent when the lake opened in 1993, and subsequent years show that action is best early in the season before the summer heat sends fish deep. Special size, gear and limit restrictions are in effect to protect this unusual fishery. A boat launch and facilities, including hiking trails, have been constructed by the U.S. Forest Service. Call the U.S.F.S. for information (206) 247-5473.

Horseshoe Lake - This lake, of 80 acres, is located in the Woodland City Park. In addition to heavy rainbow and brown trout plants for opening day, expect a few larger carry-over trout. Check regulations for extended season.

Kress Lake - A 30 acre spring fed lake located between I-5 and the Kalama River Road, approximately 4 miles north of the town of Kalama. Contains rainbow and brown trout. The area has facilities for wheelchair anglers and is rated handicap accessible (Level 1). It is questionable whether the paths to fishing areas are always up to accommodating wheelchairs. Boat access for car-toppers only. No internal combustion engines. Check regulations for strict size (slot) limits on the largemouth bass inhabiting the lake.

Merrill Lake - A fly fishing only lake containing a successfully established population of brown trout. Located north of the town of Cougar. Check regulations for catch and maximum size limits on trout.

Sacajewea Lake - An elongated, 48 acre lake in the city of Longview. Known for excellent largemouth bass and bluegill fishing, it is also stocked with rainbow and brown trout. Limited to electric motors, and these can be used only after obtaining a permit from the Longview Parks Department.

Yale Lake (Reservoir) - This big impoundment on the Lewis River near the town of Cougar, contains a large population of kokanee. The WDFW often provides a bonus catch limit in years when the kokanee are abundant. Cutthroat trout can be caught in the Siouxon Creek arm.

DOUGLAS COUNTY

Grimes Lake - An alkaline lake, Grimes is stocked with Lahontan cutthroat trout. A favorite with fly fishers, this selective fishery is available in a short season. Fish average 3 pounds, with best action in June and July. Check regulations for catch limit (usually 1 trout).

Jameson Lake - A popular lake that is usually stocked with rainbow trout fry that can be caught as yearlings. Good fishing depends upon survival of previous years fry plants, so Jameson can be inconsistent. Check regs. for split season.

FERRY COUNTY

(Franklin D.) Roosevelt Lake - This major water recreation area of 79,000 average acres, originated with the construction of Grand Coulee Dam in 1941. While it contains virtually all fish species found in Washington, a big attraction are large rainbow trout and kokanee. Due to fluctuation in water levels which disrupts natural trout reproduction, the state has developed cooperative net-pen rearing projects to supplement catches. A good place to try for rainbow trout is the area from Keller Ferry south west four miles. Check regulations for maximum catch and size limits on trout. Walleye are also caught here, so be sure of the slot limit and season on this species as well.

Curlew Lake - Located in a state park, via Highway 21, ten miles north of Republic. Spring and early summer fishing for stocked rainbow trout can be excellent trolling a fly or lure below the surface at various depths. Some large carry-over rainbows as well. Good state park facilities.

Davis Lake - A 14 acre lake located in the Colville National Forest west of Highway 395 and the town of Boyds. Inhabited by cutthroat trout yearlings (9 - 12 inches) established from annual fry plants.

Empire Lakes - 3 small lakes (biggest 4 acres) in the Colville National Forest between the headwaters of Bacon and Emanuel Creeks, northwest of Curlew Lake. Contain small eastern brook trout.

Ferry Lake - A 19 acre lake, 9 miles south of Republic. Contains catchable size rainbow trout that have to be planted annually, due to winter kills.

Fish Lake - A little alpine lake containing catchable size rainbow trout. Located just south of Ferry Lake.

Long Lake - A 14 acre fly fishing only lake southwest of Republic in the Scatter Creek drainage. Contains cutthroat trout 9 to 16 inches. Forest service boat launch, motors restricted.

Swan Lake - A higher elevation (3,641 feet) Scatter Creek drainage lake, southwest of Republic. Contains eastern brook trout 9 - 13 inches developed from annual fry plants.

Trout Lake - This 8 acre lake, located west of Kettle Falls is inhabited by rainbow trout and can produce nice size fish early in the season.

Ward Lake - A 7 acre lake, north of Republic, which contains eastern brook trout.

GRANT COUNTY

Banks Lake - Known as the premier Walleye spot in Washington, Banks was a tremendous producer of small kokanee in early summers, particularly at the south end of the lake.

A bright Eastern Washington rainbow.

During the late 1980's this fishery declined due to a short supply of kokanee for stocking. With resumed plants fishing should improve.

Blue Lake - A good rainbow trout lake southwest of Sun Lakes State Park off Highway 17. Try also Park Lake to the north.

Dry Falls Lake - A lake of beautiful geological formation offering very good rainbow and brown trout action in the spring and fall. Located in Sun Lakes State Park. Popular with fly fishermen seeking large trout to 21 inches in some years. No boat launch, so most anglers use a float tube. Selective fishery regulations. Camping available in nearby State Park.

Lenice Lake - Located in the Crab Creek Wildlife Area (via Highway 243 southeast of Vantage) Lenice is part of a chain that includes Merry and Nunnally lakes. Fry planted rainbow trout average 15 inches, with fish in the 20 inch range not uncommon. Brown trout inhabit Lenice and Nunnally also. Access to Lenice Lake is about a half mile on foot from the sandy parking area. All three lakes are popular with northwest fly fishermen. These desert lakes can be especially good at night, and most anglers sing a tune on the hike back to camp to warn rattlesnakes of their approach along the uneven, dark trail. Selective fishery regulations apply and only rough, unimproved camp areas with pit toilets exist. An oasis of desert scenery complete with freshwater turtles, brightly colored birds, and howling coyotes.

Lenore Lake - A large, 1,670 acre lake located off Highway 17, north of the town of Soap Lake. Lenore is famous for trophy Lahontan cutthroat trout, averaging 2 to 4 pounds. Special season and selective fishery regulations are usually in effect. Best fishing is in the spring, when the water temperature is cool and the big cutthroat have not become lethargic.

Potholes Reservoir - Although considered to be primarily a bass and walleye lake, Potholes can produce large rainbow trout. Most are taken bait-fishing or trolling lures during spring and early summer. The Mar-Don Resort and O'Sullivan Dam areas at the south end are good places to start.

Quincy Wildlife Area Lakes - Located 8 miles south of the town of Quincy, are two rainbow trout lakes; Burke and Quincy. Fish them early in the season.

Rocky Ford Creek and Ponds - A fly fishing-only stream, Rocky Ford deserves mention due to its slow meandering character, similar to a still water fishery. The upper mile is on Dept. of Fish and Wildlife Land and often provides the best fishing for large, sometimes wary, rainbow trout. Light tippets and delicate presentations are necessary. Wading is not allowed, and the rule is strictly enforced. This special little area is a rich fresh water environment with an abundance of aquatic insects.

Seep Lakes - The name of these small lakes, in the area below O'Sullivan Dam, first applied to several ponds which formed in 1954 by seepage from Potholes Reservoir. Later, individual names were given such as Windmill, Canal, Pit, Teal and Hampton. Most of the lakes are walk-in access, but a few such as Windmill have rough boat launches. The WDFW has had problems here with illegally introduced warmwater species that compete with the stocked trout. Several of these lakes traditionally open early, on March 1. Fun to hike from lake to lake, with great desert landscapes.

GRAYS HARBOR COUNTY

Lake Aberdeen - A 63 acre lake, just north of Highway 12. Usually crowded on opening day, it produces stocked rainbows and an occasional carry-over rainbow or cutthroat.

Klone Lakes - Small lakes (Klone, Discovery, Bone) north of Wynoochee Reservoir, in the Olympic National Forest offer hike-in fishing. They are planted with trout every 3 to 4 years.

Satsop Lakes - Two little lakes at 2500 foot elevation in the Olympic National Forest west of Wynoochee Reservoir near the Mason County line. Small cutthroat trout can be found here. A walk-in is required.

Sylvia Lake - Located in a State Park, one mile north of Montesano. This 32 acre lake offers good fishing for small rainbow trout at the beginning of the season. Sometimes receives additional trout plants in June.

ISLAND COUNTY

Cranberry Lake - Located in spectacular Deception Pass State Park. Fair rainbow trout fishing, with a few brown trout . Some bass and perch as well. Tough to find solitude on a crowded summer weekend here.

Deer Lake - Just one mile west of Clinton on Whidbey Island, and surrounded by new development, this 82 acre lake can provide good fishing for both rainbow and cutthroat trout early in the season.

Goss Lake - Located near the quaint town of Langley on Whidbey Island. Goss has a WDFW access at the east end of the lake. Rainbow and cutthroat trout are present.

Lone Lake - Located between Freeland and Langley, it contains stocked rainbow trout and some large carry-over fish. WDFW access on the north shore.

JEFFERSON COUNTY

Anderson Lake - This 68 acre lake is located in Anderson Lake State Park, 1 1/2 miles off Highway 20 and about 9 miles south of Port Townsend. Fishing for rainbow trout to 3 pounds can be excellent here, with the average 12 inches. No internal combustion engines. Check current regulations for selective fishery regulations / catch and release period from Sept. 1 to Oct. 31.

Devil's Lake - A small lake 2 miles south of Quilcene that contains cutthroat trout to 11 inches. Poor road access to lake.

Horseshoe Lake - A 13 acre rainbow trout lake southwest of Port Ludlow off Highway 104.

Leland Lake - Early season fishing is usually good for rainbow trout to 12 inches on this 100 acre lake on Highway 101 north of Quilcene. Try in the fall for larger rainbows.

Tarboo Lake - This 24 acre lake 9 miles west of Port Ludlow offers stocked rainbow trout from 9 to 11 inches. A few larger, carry-over trout are present to make things interesting.

KING COUNTY

Alice Lake - A 22 acre lake just south of Fall City, containing rainbow and eastern brook trout.

Angle Lake - Located 2 miles south of Sea-Tac airport off Highway 99, this 100 acre suburban lake receives plants of rainbow trout in the spring. County park with facilities.

Boyle, Bridges and Klaus Lakes - Located on Weyerhaeuser property 4 miles northeast of Snoqualmie Falls are these interconnected lakes of 24 - 60 acres. Managed for native cutthroat trout, with selective fishery regulations in effect on all species. Inlet and outlet streams may be closed waters.

Calligan Lake - A 310 acre lake accessed from the Weyerhaeuser Snoqualmie Tree Farm, 9 miles north east of the town of North Bend. Contains wild rainbow, cutthroat and eastern brook trout that can be quite large. Popular with fly fishermen. Small boat, canoe or float tube access. Late season closures may be in effect due to fire danger.

Deep Lake - 6 miles northeast of Enumclaw in Nolte State Park, this 39 acre lake contains rainbow trout, cutthroat trout and kokanee. Nature trails, swimming beach and picnic area too!

Green Lake - Located in the heart of Seattle, Green is usually stocked with several thousand catchable rainbow trout in the spring. Some brown trout are present along with species from bass to carp.

Hull Lake - This 6 acre, beaver pond type lake is located in a quiet forest setting within the Weyerhaeuser tree farm, 9 miles north of Snoqualmie in the East Fork Griffin Creek drainage. It is managed for stocked cutthroat trout.

Langlois Lake - A rainbow trout lake, 1 mile southeast of the town of Carnation.

Margaret Lake - A 44 acre lake with public access and boat ramp, 4 miles northeast of Duvall. It contains rainbow trout and a few cutthroat.

McLeod Lake - Located 5 miles north of the town of North Bend off the county road along the North Fork Snoqualmie River. A walk-in lake, containing rainbow, cutthroat and eastern brook trout.

Moss Lake - Moss is located 3 miles north of the town of Carnation off the Kelly / Stillwater Road. There is a primitive access on the south shore for float tubes or small car-topper boat. Contains native cutthroat trout.

Ravensdale Lake - An 18 acre lake just west of Ravensdale. Offers float tube, car-topper boat or bank fishing access only. Contains native cutthroat trout. Check the selective fishery regulations, bait restrictions, and size / catch limits.

Lake Sammamish - A large lake surrounded by beautiful homes 4 miles east of Bellevue. The state park on the south shore provides public access and facilities, including a boat launch. Known for wild cutthroat trout and smallmouth bass.

Shady Lake - This 21 acre lake is located between Renton and Maple Valley, west of Highway 169. It is managed for rainbow and cutthroat trout, but is often crowded. Check for late season opening date and catch limit on trout over 14 inches.

Sunday Lake - Located 13 miles northeast of North Bend within the Alpine Lakes Wilderness in the north fork drainage of the Snoqualmie River. This 21 acre lake produces relatively large cutthroat trout to the fly, particularly in late summer. A hike-in and fording of Sunday Creek (closed to fishing) is required. Best fished from a float tube or small inflatable.

Walker Lake - A lake of 11 Acres near the town of Cumberland. Has a WDFW boat ramp on the south shore and contains rainbow and cutthroat trout.

Lake Washington - Although this huge metropolitan lake lies between sprawling Seattle and Bellevue, it holds many species of fish, including rainbow and cutthroat trout. Fishing piers, parks and public boat access dot the shoreline among much private property. As a side note, don't disregard the good population of largemouth and smallmouth bass that lurk around pilings and docks. Check current regulations for special seasons and catch / size limits per species.

Wilderness Lake - A 67 acre lake with a WDFW boat ramp that lies just south of Maple Valley. It contains stocked rainbow trout and kokanee and is situated within a county park.

KITSAP COUNTY

Buck Lake - A 20 acre lake that is located near the tip of the Kitsap peninsula south of Hansville. Contains rainbow trout and can be crowded on opening day.

Horseshoe Lake - A 40 acre lake containing stocked rainbows, located 9 miles south of Port Orchard.

Kitsap Lake - This 240 acre lake just outside of Bremerton contains rainbow trout, cutthroat trout, and largemouth bass as well.

Mission Lake - Mission lies 8 miles west of Bremerton and contains planted rainbow trout.

Wildcat Lake - Located 6 miles northwest of Bremerton off the Seabeck Highway. A 112 acre lake providing good fishing for rainbow trout, cutthroat and some coho. The WDFW has reportedly stocked 3 to 6 pound adult steelhead here.

KITTITAS COUNTY

Cle Elum Lake - A large storage reservoir that is a fair producer of kokanee.

Cooper Lake - This higher elevation lake, 4 miles west of the town of Salmon-La-Sac, is a consistent producer of small brook trout and rainbow trout, in addition to a few kokanee. Although there is a boat launch, gasoline motors are prohibited.

Easton Lake - Located in a state park outside the town of Easton, off I-90, this 230 acre lake provides fair fishing for stocked rainbow trout.

Fiorito Lake - A 54 acre lake southeast of Ellensberg, on I-82. Good fishing can be had for rainbow and brown trout to 14 inches. Rated handicapped accessibility - level 1. Amenities listed include black top trails to lake for wheelchairs. No internal combustion motors.

Fish Lake - A slough-like lake on the upper Cle Elum River, containing brook trout and a few rainbows. Check special regulations for size and catch limits.

Hyas Lake - Located above Fish lake in the headwaters of the Cle Elem River, it contains brook trout. Fishing can be good from July through September for trout to 14 inches. A trail hike is required to reach Hyas.

Kachess Lake - Early summer fishing for small kokanee and some rainbow trout can be found on this popular recreation reservoir off I-90. There is often a bonus catch limit on kokanee but restricted size / catch limits for trout.

Keechelus Lake - Fishing can be good here for 10 - 12 inch kokanee during the months of May and June. Reported poor boat launching after reservoir is drawn down in summer. To reach the lake take the Hyak exit from I-90, about 4 miles south east of Snoqualmie Pass. Check current regulations for size / catch limits.

Lost Lake - Although there are a dozen "Lost Lakes" in

Eastern Washington, this 145 acre "Lost" is Located west of Keechelus Lake, and contains brook trout averaging 9 inches, with a few larger fish reported.

Manashtash Lake - A 23 acre high country lake 19 miles west of the town of Ellensburg. Can be accessible by four wheel drive in late May, it is a consistent producer of eastern brook trout, that have been stocked there since 1957. Heavy algae blooms in summer can slow fishing.

Yakima River - Considered by many fly fishers to be the best resident trout stream in Washington, The Yakima's reputation demands that we mention it, notwithstanding the scope of this book as a guide to lakes. The Section between Roza and Easton Dams is now open all year, with selective fishery regulations in effect. Fly fishing is best in early spring and again in September and October for wild rainbows that average 12 inches, but can be much larger. Check current regulations closely for rules pertaining to each species.

KLICKITAT COUNTY

Horsethief Lake - A 92 acre lake formed in 1956 by backwaters of The Dalles Dam. It is located within a state park between the Columbia River and Highway 14. Horsethief usually receives a healthy quantity of catchable size rainbow trout prior to opening day, often augmented by supplemental plantings in May and June. The park provides good boat launch, camping and picnic facilities.

Rowland Lakes - Once an arm of the Columbia River 4 miles east of Bingen. The original lake, called DuBois by locals, was created by fill when the railroad was constructed here. Well stocked with rainbow and eastern brook trout. Public boat launch on North Rowland.

Spearfish Lake - A popular spot when the season opens, the lake contains catchable size rainbows plus some large brood-stock trout. Great shore access for bank anglers. Spearfish, formed in the 1950's by seepage from the Dalles Dam, one mile to the south, is 22 acres and has a boat ramp.

LEWIS COUNTY

Borst Pond - A Juvenile only lake (anglers 14 years or younger) that is well stocked with rainbow trout for the early season. Located west of Centralia on the old Borst Family Homestead, dating back to the 1850's.

Carlisle Lake - Usually open until the end of February, this 20 acre lake near Onalaska receives generous quantities of catchable size rainbow and brown trout from the WDFW. A large-mouth bass fishery is being established here, so be aware of minimum size limits for this species and check current regulations. No internal combustion engines allowed.

Mayfield Lake - The big attraction at Mayfield is the recently introduced tiger musky. This northern pike - muskellunge cross is fished in the warm summer months with plugs or bucktail spinners and can reach in excess of 20 pounds. The musky's presence should literally eat into the lake's squawfish population and help to improve the rainbow trout and landlocked coho salmon fishery. Located on Highway 12, 15 miles east of I-5.

Mineral Lake - Located in the shadow of Mt Rainier off Highway 7 before it crosses the Nisqually River, this 277 acre lake has received plants of 100,000 fingerling rainbow trout every 3 years. The WDFW also puts rainbow trout broodstock and brown trout into the lake. Some handicapped facilities.

Riffe Lake - A large reservoir on the Cowlitz River that contains brown, rainbow and cutthroat trout. Riffe is also the recipient of landlocked coho salmon. The name "silver trout" is more appropriate for these fish than the kokanee (which evolved from the sockeye salmon). Coho in Riffe average 10 - 16 inches and anglers must have a Personal Use License to catch and retain these fish. See your license dealer.

LINCOLN COUNTY

Deer Springs Lake - Rainbow trout are planted annually in this 60 acre lake located 12 miles northeast of Odessa. Also known as Deer Lake, check the regulations for early closure.

Fishtrap Lake - Located east of Sprague off I-90, Fishtrap is a long, narrow lake with a boat launch at the north end. It is planted consistently with rainbow trout fry and traditionally provides the best opening day catch rate in the region.

MASON COUNTY

Aldrich Lake - A 10 acre lake containing stocked rainbows, located 2 miles south of Dewatto.

Benson Lake - Fair fishing for 9 to 11 inch cutthroat and rainbow trout. Located 9 miles southwest of Belfair off the Mason-Benson Road.

Cady Lake - A 15 acre fly fishing only lake inhabited by 7 - 13 inch cutthroat trout. Also receives a small plant of catchable-size rainbows annually. Check regulations for trout catch limit (usually 2).

Clara Lake - Shown on most maps as Don Lake, it is located between Aldrich and Cady Lakes, south of Dewatto. Contains 7 - 9 inch rainbow trout.

Lake Cushman - The Large reservoir 4 miles northwest of Hoodsport offers kokanee fishing in the summer and good late season fishing for cutthroat trout. Dolly varden are present and may be subject to a closed season, so check current regulations.

Devereaux Lake - A 94 acre lake planted with rainbows that contains a few trout to 4 pounds. Good for kokanee in the summer. Located just northwest of Allyn.

Haven Lake - 7 miles west of Belfair is this 69 acre lake offering good fishing for rainbow and cutthroat trout.

Isabella Lake - Located 2 miles south of Shelton off Highway 101, this 200 acre lake provides fair year-round fishing for rainbow trout. A state boat access is available.

Island Lake - The main quarry in this 109 acre lake are largemouth and smallmouth bass, however a few large rainbows trout are present. Island is located north of the town of Shelton.

Melbourne Lake - A good destination for taking cutthroat trout to 14 inches , especially in the fall. This 35 acre lake is located 3 miles north of the town of Lilliwaup.

Price's Lake - A 110 acre catch and release lake with selective fishery regulations imposed. Noted as an excellent fly fishing lake for large rainbows, cutthroat and brook trout. Located between Lake Cushman and Hood Canal, about a mile from the Olympic National Forest boundary.

Robbins Lake - This small lake south of Dewatto offers good fishing for planted rainbow trout.

Spencer Lake - Located 7 miles northeast of Shelton off

Highway 3, this 230 acre lake offers good rainbow trout fishing that holds up through fall. As a side note, Spencer provides excellent largemouth bass fishing in the hot summer months. State boat launch facilities.

Tiger Lake - Smaller rainbow trout and some nice carry-overs are available at this 109 acre lake that lies on the Kitsap-Mason County line. State access facilities.

Wildberry Lake - Located 2 miles northwest of Tahuya and the bend of Hood Canal is this little lake containing rainbow trout.

Wooten Lake - 7 miles west of Belfair lies this 68 acre lake inhabited by rainbow and cutthroat trout. A state access is available.

OKANOGAN COUNTY

Aeneas Lake - A 27 acre fly fishing only lake that is stocked annually and contains a good number of large carry-over rainbow trout. It is located west of Highway 97 and the town of Tonasket. Car-topper boats or float tubes can be launched.

Alta Lake - Good rainbow trout fishing can be had at Alta, 2 miles southwest of the town of Pateros.

Big Twin Lake - Some nice rainbows inhabit this 79 acre lake in the Methow Valley, 2 miles south of Winthrop. Selective fishery regulations and a catch limit apply.

Blue Lake - At the head of the Sinlahekin Valley, this 160 acre lake was created by a dam built in 1923, which inundated the original Blue Lake, Long Lake, and Round Lake. Check for selective fishery regulations and special catch limits on the rainbow trout that run 12 to 16 inches here.

Chopaka Lake — Okanogan County, on a windy day.

49

Bonapart Lake - Located in the Okanogan National Forest about 20 miles east of Tonasket, this lake is known for it's big mackinaw that are taken early in the morning or late in the evening, mostly by trollers. It is stocked with rainbow and brook trout as well.

Chopaka Lake - Chopaka is a fly fishing only lake that sits in a high valley 7 miles south of the Canadian border, north of the town of Loomis. Well known for it's spring *Callibaetis* mayfly hatches, fishing can be very good for large rainbows or can quickly halt due to a brisk wind. The steep road-in is poor during the rainy season. A limited number of campsites exist (watch for rattlesnakes). No boat motors allowed.

Conconully Lake - This popular recreation spot in the hills north of Omak, and the adjoining reservoir, provide good fishing for 9 to 10 inch rainbow trout, plus a few larger ones.

Ell Lake - Due to a re-occurring water level problem, an aerator has been installed at "L" to provide more oxygen to the rainbow trout that inhabit this 21 acre lake sitting in a glacial kettle, 16 miles southeast of Tonasket. Follow Highway 20 to the Aeneas Valley Road. Fishing can be very good here for 12 inch plus trout. Selective fishery regulations.

Fish Lake - Located 5 miles northeast of Conconully, this 102 acre lake contains planted rainbow trout with some nice carry-overs in most years. There are 13 "Fish Lakes" in eastern Washington; this one is partially in the Sinlahekin Wildlife Area.

Forde Lake - A 24 acre lake, stocked with brook trout, in the Sinlahekin Wildlife Area.

High Lakes - There are over 125 alpine lakes in Okanogan County. Most are either stocked with trout or have natural reproducing populations. Fishing can be excellent after snow melt from July through October for primarily cutthroat trout, and some rainbow or brook trout.

Leader Lake - This 169 acre reservoir was created in 1910 when a dam was placed on the natural lake (about half the present size). Heavy irrigation demands task the lake during the summer, so trout survival can be affected. Expect fair to good fishing, nevertheless, for chunky rainbows averaging 12 inches most years. Located off Highway 20, due west from the town of Okanogan.

Patterson Lake - Located in the Methow Wildlife Area west of Winthrop, this popular 130 acre lake, with good facilities, contains stocked rainbow trout and some older rainbows up to 15 inches. Also provides good fly fishing, in some years, for eastern brook trout at the south end of the lake.

Pearrygin Lake - Good fishing can usually be found for rainbow trout on this 200 acre lake in the Upper Methow Valley at a state park. The park is approximately 5 miles north of Winthrop, and has excellent facilities.

Rat Lake - A rainbow trout lake that has an unusual winter season (December - March). Check current state regulations. Located 6 miles north of Brewster.

Sidley Lake - Just outside of Molson and a mile below the Canadian border lies this 116 acre lake which can provide good fishing for rainbow trout 12 to 17 inches.

Spectacle Lake - A popular vacation spot, Spectacle contains rainbow trout. It is located 9 miles northwest of Tonasket, and was originally two lakes, giving the appearance of a pair of eye glasses - thus the name. Several resorts as well as public facilities. Check current regulations for season dates and catch / possession limits.

Wannacut Lake - A 411 acre lake, 6 miles southwest of Oroville. It contains rainbow trout and a few Lahonton cutthroat. Curiously, the lake is slightly saline, due to concentrations of Epsom salts in the area. Sun Cove Resort and a public access provide launching for boats.

PACIFIC COUNTY

Loomis Lake - This narrow lake containing rainbow trout is located on the Long Beach Peninsula.

Pacific County Ponds - Many small ponds throughout the county are stocked with cutthroat. Check local sources for info.

PEND OREILLE COUNTY

Brown's Lake - Cutthroat trout run 8 to 12 inches at this fly fishing only lake, 13 miles northeast of the town of Usk. A Forest Service campground and small boat launch (no motors) exist on the south shore.

Carl's Lake - A 20 acre lake southwest of Tiger, shown on some maps as Brown's Lake. Hard to reach without four wheel drive, but containing eastern brook trout 10 - 14 inches.

Crescent Lake - A 22 acre lake planted with rainbow trout fry, located 9 miles north of Metaline Falls off highway 31, one mile south of the Canadian border.

Fan Lake - Planted annually with cutthroat and rainbow trout, this 73 acre lake is located 8 miles northeast of the town of Deer Park. Check for early closer and engine restrictions.

Frater Lake - Northernmost in the Little Pend Oreille Chain of Lakes, southwest of Ione. Inhabited by 9 to 13 inch cutthroat trout.

Half Moon Lake - A small, alpine lake in the Kaniksu National Forest northeast of Usk. Originally called New Moon Lake, it provides good fishing for small, wild brook trout in spring and fall.

Leo Lake - A cutthroat trout lake of 39 acres just south of Frater Lake.

Marshall Lake - Planted annually with cutthroat trout finger-lings, this 189 acre lake lies in a beautiful part of the county, near the Idaho border north of Newport. Boat access through a resort and public area.

Muskegon Lake - AkA Moss Keg Lake, at 8 acres it harbors some good size cutthroat trout. It is located next to the Idaho border, 16 miles east of Metaline Falls.

Nile Lake - Eastern brook trout from 8 - 14 inches and an occasional rainbow are caught at this 23 acre lake off Highway 20, a few miles southwest of the town of Tiger.

Petit Lake - This 11 acre lake on the northwest side of Diamond Peak, contains cutthroat trout. Located up the East Fork LeClerc Creek Road from the town of Ruby.

Sacheen Lake - Heavy annual plants of eastern brook and rainbow trout, account for the fishing opportunities on this 282 acre lake, 12 miles southwest of Newport.

Skookum Lakes - Located 7 miles north of Usk, these two lakes contain some nice eastern brook trout to 11 inches.

Sullivan Lake - A natural lake (increased in size by a dam built in 1931), Sullivan has produced large brown trout. Small kokanee and an occasional rainbow or cutthroat trout are also available from this big lake in the Colville National Forest.

PIERCE COUNTY

American Lake - Located 8 miles southwest of Tacoma, near Fort Lewis. Facilities include two county parks and a state boat ramp. Stocked rainbow trout and kokanee.

Carney Lake - Sitting on the Pierce-Kitsap County line, 4 miles north of Vaughn, is this 39 acre rainbow trout lake.

Clear Lake - The primary species are rainbow trout and kokanee at this 155 acre lake, 4 miles north of Eatonville. Trout fishing is best here, early in the season.

Harts Lake - Planted annually with catchable size rainbow trout, this 109 acre lake provides early season trout action. A good largemouth bass fishery exists here, but slot-size limits are imposed. Check current regulations. Harts is open all year and lies 7 miles southeast of Yelm.

Kapowsin Lake - Located between Orting and Eatonville, this year round lake receives annual spring plants of rainbow trout. Good bank access along the west shoreline. Good summer bass fishing, but check regulations for slot-size limits.

Ohop Lake - Annual spring rainbow trout plants provide good early season fishing. State boat ramp area on south shore, with bank access along the county road for non-boaters. Pan fish and bass also available when the trout fishing slows down later in the summer. Check size limits on largemouth bass.

Rapjohn Lake - Planted annually with rainbow and sometimes brown trout. Good bass and pan fish action can be had in the warmer months. Check bass fishing special regulations. This 55 acre lake is located 4 miles northwest of Eatonville, and has a state boat ramp on the west shore.

Spanaway Lake - A very popular destination, this 262 acre lake is located 10 miles south of Tacoma off Highway 7. A county park provides boating and bank fishing access. Primary species are rainbow trout, bass, perch, and some crappie.

Tanwax Lake - A 173 acre lake near Eatonville. State facilities and two resorts provide boat access. Fishing can be good here for rainbow trout 10 to 13 inches. Best trout action is in the spring and fall. A slot-size limit may be in effect on largemouth bass inhabiting the lake, so check current regulations.

SAN JUAN COUNTY

Cascade Lake - Located in Moran State Park, on Orcas Island, this 171 acre lake has become a popular opening day spot. Fly fishing can be good in the spring, and holds up well into June, for rainbow trout and cutthroat trout. Kokanee inhabit Cascade as well. State park boat access and swimming beach facilities.

Egg Lake - Fishing can be good for rainbow trout in this 7 acre lake on the northwest end of San Juan Island.

Hummel Lake - A trout and bass lake found at the north end of Lopez Island. Minimum size limits have been imposed on largemouth bass in the past, so check current regulations each year.

Mountain Lake - Located in Moran State Park on Orcas Island. It is the largest body of fresh water in the county. Kokanee fishing can be good, near the surface, on lure or fly during May, early June, and again in the fall. They go deep in the hot summer months. A few cutthroat and brook trout are available.

Sportsmans Lake - Located on the way to Roach Harbor on San Juan Island, this 66 acre lake is primarily thought of as largemouth bass water, but a few cutthroat trout swim here as well.

SKAGIT COUNTY

Beaver Lake - Located one mile from Clear Lake, Beaver is better known for it's summer bass and crappie fishing.

Big Lake - Just east of the growing town of Mt. Vernon, Big has a good reputation for largemouth bass fishing. Some large cutthroat are caught on occasion. Special slot limits may be in effect for bass, so check current regulations.

Campbell Lake - 5 miles north of Anacortes lies this 410 acre lake that is well known for it's spiny-ray fishing. Check regulations for size-slot limit on bass. Open all year, Campbell offers early season rainbow and cutthroat trout action as well. Some handicapped facilities.

Lake Cavanaugh - Located 10 miles northeast of Arlington, this 844 acre lake produces good trout and kokanee fishing in May and June.

Clear Lake - A very popular opening day spot, 3 miles south of the town of Sedro Woolley, it is stocked with rainbow trout. As a side note; some good crappie fishing available during the summer.

Day Lake - Accessed by logging road, this 136 acre lake south of Hamilton produces good catches of rainbow and eastern brook trout in June and then again in the fall.

Beautiful Pass Lake on Fidalgo Island is a favorite destination for Western Washington Fly fishermen.

Erie Lake - An excellent opening day lake, 4 miles south of Anacortes on Fidalgo Island. One of the better average rainbow trout catch rates in the region.

Granite Lakes - A chance to catch grayling in Big Granite is the incentive for anglers to hike into these Cascade lakes, at the head of Boulder Creek. Also contain cutthroat to 14 inches. Strict catch and release regulations apply to the grayling.

Heart Lake - This nice, 61 acre lake, outside of Anacortes, is consistent in the early season for rainbow trout. Expect big crowds opening week.

High Lakes - Backpackers are aware of the good size twin lakes variety of cutthroat trout that inhabit many of the alpine lakes in the North Cascades and Skagit County. Some lakes are stocked occasionally, while others populate by natural reproduction. A few offer rainbow trout.

McMurray Lake - Annual plants of rainbow trout account for the traditionally good early season here. Some cutthroat trout, perch and black crappie too.

Pass Lake - A beautiful still-water fishery on Fidalgo Island near Deception Pass. This 98 acre lake is fly fishing only and a popular destination for float tubers in the spring. The Fidalgo Flyfishers monitor the lake for species data. Big rainbow trout, cutthroat and brown trout, as well as Atlantic salmon are the quarry. Check regulations annually.

Shannon Lake - This large impoundment north of Concrete can provide good kokanee fishing. Special size restrictions may be in effect.

Sixteen Lake - Great early season fishing for stocked rainbow trout can be found most years at this 41 acre lake, east of Conway.

Ten Lake - There is hiking trail access to this 16 acre lake, 4 miles northeast of Conway. Rainbow, cutthroat, and brook trout inhabit Ten.

SKAMANIA COUNTY

Kidney Lake - A 12 acre lake with no developed access, north of North Bonneville, that is stocked with rainbow trout annually.

Little Ashes Lake - Off Highway 14 west of Stevenson, this small lake is stocked annually with rainbow trout. A few bass are present.

Swift Reservoir - In some years, up to one million fingerling rainbow trout have been planted in this 10 mile-long reservoir on the North Fork of the Lewis River. Springtime finds the fish congregating around the dam and inlet streams, but by June they are caught throughout the reservoir.

Tunnel Lake - A 13 acre lake off the Lewis and Clark Highway (14) between the Columbia River towns of Cook and Underwood. Good opening week action can usually be found as a result of annual plants of catchable-size rainbow trout. No boat ramp, but car top boats can be carried to the water. Some bass and perch fishing in the warm months.

SNOHOMISH COUNTY

Armstrong Lake - Fair spring fishing is available for rainbow and cutthroat trout at this 31 acre lake a few miles north of Arlington. State access on the south shore.

Blackman's Lake - Located in the heart of Snohomish, a town known more for it's antique shops. This 60 acre lake contains rainbow and cutthroat trout and is best for these species in the spring or fall. Some bass and perch on hot summer days. A handicapped access fishing pier extends from the northeast shore.

Bosworth Lake - Bosworth lies south of Granite Falls and contains rainbow and cutthroat trout. State boat access.

Cassidy Lake - A good bass and panfish lake east of Marysville, Cassidy also contains rainbow trout. Check regulations for possible slot-size limits on largemouth bass.

Chain Lake - This 23 acre lake, north of Monroe, is inhabited by rainbow and cutthroat trout. A primitive access exists on the south shore.

Crabapple Lake - A 36 acre lake, 7 miles northwest of Marysville. Contains rainbow trout and has a state access on the north shore.

Echo Lake - Managed for rainbow trout, Echo covers 16 acres and is located off Highway 522 near Maltby. State access.

Flowing Lake - Located within a county park, 6 miles north of Monroe. Good boat launch and shore fishing access. State rated handicapped accessible - level 1, including wheelchair camping, trails, and picnic area, as well as fishing facilities. Contains rainbow trout and largemouth bass.

Goodwin Lake - Situated in Wenberg State Park, between Marysville and Stanwood. Goodwin is a mixed species lake, with rainbow (stocked in the spring) and cutthroat trout, both largemouth and smallmouth bass, crappie, perch and sunfish.

Ketchum Lake - Rainbow trout are stocked in this 19 acre lake, located 3 miles north of Stanwood.

Ki Lake - Located about a mile east of Goodwin Lake, Ki provides good rainbow trout fishing in the early season.

Lost Lake - Annual rainbow trout plants, and some cutthroat trout are available at this small lake east of Maltby, off Highway 522. Best fishing in late spring.

Martha Lake - Also known as Warm Beach Lake, this 58 acre lake is located 10 miles northwest of Marysville. It contains both rainbow and cutthroat trout.

Panther Lake - A 47 acre mixed species lake, 5 miles northeast of Snohomish, just west of Flowing Lake Park.

Roesiger Lake - Located in a county park, northeast of Snohomish, it contains rainbow trout, kokanee and spiny rays. A fishing pier extends from the park.

Serene Lake - Off Highway 99 at Shelby Road in the city of Lynnwood. Stocked with rainbow trout.

Silver Lake - Lies 5 miles south of Everett, and has a city park on the west shore. Contains rainbow trout, cutthroat trout, and kokanee. No developed boat ramp.

Spada Lake - A good fly fishing lake for rainbow and cut-throat trout. Located 8 miles north of Sultan. Selective fishery regulations may apply, check with Washington Dept. of Fish and Wildlife region 4 office, in Mill Creek at (206) 775 - 1311. Internal combustion engines prohibited.

Stevens Lake - A large, natural lake, Stevens has boat launch facilities and a pier in the county park off Davies Road, 6 miles east of Everett. Open year round, the lake contains some cut-throat and rainbow trout, with fishing for these species best in fall. Kokanee fishing can be good from May - August. Also inhabited by bass, yellow perch and catfish. Handicapped accessible including wheelchair docks.

Storm Lake - This 78 acre lake, about 5 miles north of Monroe, contains rainbow trout and a few larger cutthroat.

A LISTING OF WASHINGTON TROUT LAKES

SPOKANE COUNTY

Amber Lake - Rainbow and cutthroat trout create a quality fishery at this 117 acre lake, 11 miles south west of Cheney. Selective fishery regulations and a special late season catch and release policy apply. Low water levels may effect boat launch capabilities.

Badger Lake - A long, narrow lake amidst basalt cliffs that contains fry planted rainbow trout. Badger is known for it's mayfly hatches which provide great fly fishing in some years. A few problems, such as low water and illegal introduction of largemouth bass (predators of rainbow trout fry), may effect trout survival. Handicapped accessibility is rated very good.

Chapman Lake - A good rainbow trout and kokanee lake south of Cheney, Chapman also harbors large and smallmouth black bass.

Clear Lake - One of seven "Clear Lakes" in eastern Washington, this Clear is located 2 miles south of the town of Medical Lake. Stocked annually with catchable size rainbow and brown trout, along with supplemental fall fry plants.

Fish Lake - A 47 acre lake located northeast of Cheney on the Cheney-Spokane Highway. Eastern brook trout fishing can be good here some years. No internal combustion engines.

Liberty Lake - Located in the town of the same name, Liberty has strong populations of bass and perch, but has been planted with rainbow and brown trout.

Medical Lake - This 149 acre lake is open during a short season in compliance with local ordinances of the town of Medical Lake. Brown trout are stocked here regularly, with fish in the 15 inch range. Years ago, it was presumed that Medical Lake would not support fish due to a high content of organic material that depletes oxygen. Selective fishery regulations apply and motor-boats are prohibited.

Newman Lake - A large lake, east of Spokane on Highway 290. Contains a good population of rainbow and brown trout, as well as bass, catfish and crappie, which makes Newman an interesting lake to fish. A public facility on the east shore provides good wheelchair accessibility. Check current regulations for limits on tiger musky that have been planted here.

Silver Lake - Just east of the town of Medical Lake lies this 486 acre lake stocked with rainbow and brown trout. It usually contains some surplus hatchery broodstock.

West Medical Lake - Annual rainbow trout fry plants create a consistently good fishery here. In addition to West Medical Lake Resort at the south end, excellent public facilities are available. The state rates this as a highly recommended wheelchair access and fishing site, with blacktop paths to bankside. The shallow areas of the lake are popular fly fishing spots. Check regulations for possible short season.

Williams Lake - A popular rainbow trout lake supported by fry plants. Williams is a steady producer, with best fly fishing during the spring-early summer Mayfly hatches. An excellent public boat launch (fly fishing good in this area!) and two resorts can be found on the lake. Take the Mullinix Road from the west end of Cheney about 12 miles.

STEVENS COUNTY

Bayley Lake - A fly fishing-only lake, 10 miles north of Chewelah on the west side of McDonald Mountain in the Little Pend Oreille Wildlife Area. Bayley, which may be shown on older maps as "Cliff Lake", also contains catchable size rainbow trout. No motors are allowed here, with catch and release regulations in effect most years after July 4th. Check for current size/catch limits.

Black Lake - An alpine lake of 70 acres, Black can be reached by driving 15 miles east of Colville on Highway 20, then north up Gap Creek Road. This is an opportunity to fish for 8 to 12 inch eastern brook and rainbow trout in a nice setting at 3700 ft.

Cedar Lake - Rainbow trout planted from fry grow to 18 inches in this 51 acre lake, 4 miles south of the Canadian border and just north of Leadpoint. Public access is available.

Coffin Lake - Coffin is the southernmost in the Little Pend Oreille Lakes chain east of Colville. It is inhabited by most types of trout.

Deep Lake - Stocked with catchable size rainbow and cutthroat trout because the survival rate of fry plants has not good here. Located about 12 miles southeast of Northport.

Deer Lake - Although most lakes in Stevens County are relatively small, this large (1163 acre), natural lake is home to rainbow trout, a few kokanee, and some mackinaw. It is located 3 miles north of Loon Lake off Highway 395.

Elbow Lake - Located in the Colville National Forest, 12 miles west of Northport. Elbow has been planted with eastern brook trout fry for many years.

Gillette Lake - Cutthroat trout are planted in this member of the Little Pend Oreille chain of lakes. Try also Heritage Lake to the north for good cutthroat trout fishing.

Jumpoff Joe Lake - Catchable size eastern brook and brown trout are planted here, co-existing with largemouth bass and yellow perch. This 105 acre lake is located 8 miles south of Chewelah.

Loon Lake - Known for good kokanee fishing in the summer, Loon contains mixed species. Public access with some handicapped facilities and several resorts are at the lake, 28 miles north of Spokane.

McDowell Lake - Large rainbow and an occasional eastern brook trout provide great fishing at times on this fly fishing-only lake with strict catch and release regulations. Located about 12 miles southeast of Colville in the Little Pend Oreille Wildlife Area. Has a public walk-in access and no motor-boats are allowed.

Mudgett Lake - Fishing can be good in the spring for stocked rainbow trout in the 10 - 12 inch range. Mudgett is located 2 miles south of the town of Fruitland and has a public access.

Potter's Pond - Can produce large rainbow trout on opening day some years. Located just outside Colville.

Rocky Lake - A 20 acre lake 4 miles south of Colville. Planted rainbow trout fry usually run 8 - 12 inches by opening of the season.

Sherry Lake - Another in the Little Pend Oreille chain, Sherry is stocked with cutthroat trout.

Starvation Lake - Part of this 29 acre lake is in the Little Pend Oreille Wildlife Area, and it has public access with a campground. In some years, fry plants have flourished here, producing 9 - 12 inch rainbows by opening day. However, the lake often suffers from winter kill, hindering fry survival.

Thomas Lake - The largest of the Little Pend Oreille chain of lakes, Thomas offers a forest service campground and resort facilities. Planted with cutthroat trout.

Waitts Lake - Located 4 miles west of Valley on Highway 395.

This 455 acre lake was stabilized by a low dam, built in 1927. It is good mixed species water, having been planted annually with rainbow and brown trout catchables. Big largemouth bass also inhabit Waitts. Handicapped accessible.

THURSTON COUNTY

Black Lake - Some fishing for small rainbow trout is available early in the season at this 570 acre lake, 4 miles southwest of Olympia. Summer fishing heats up for cutthroat trout and bass. Handicapped accessible.

Capitol Lake - Formed by a dam across the southernmost part of Puget Sound at the mouth of the Deschutes River (Budd Inlet). A few cutthroat trout are available, along with good fall salmon fishing at this 270 acre "lake" in the city of Olympia.

Clear Lake - Good early season fishing for 9 to 13 inch rainbow and brown trout can be found, at this popular lake southeast of Yelm. Also contains cutthroat trout and largemouth bass. Big crowds on opening day. State boat launch, but limited public parking.

Deep Lake - Early season fishing can be good, in some years, for planted rainbow trout. Located in Millersylvania State Park, former pioneer homestead of the Miller family. Old growth forest and hiking trails make this a nice vacation spot. As a side note, some bass and bluegill fishing in warmer months.

Hicks Lake - This 160 acre lake is located in Lacey, and contains planted rainbows and a few large brown trout. State access and boat launch.

Long Lake - Long receives annual plants of rainbow trout and also contains a some very large brown trout. In addition, warm water species of all types thrive here. It is 330 surface acres and is located on the southeast side of the town of Lacey. Some handicapped facilities and a state boat launch are available.

McIntosh Lake - A 93 acre lake, 3 miles northeast of Tenino. It contains stocked rainbows and a few bass for summer fishing.

Offut Lake - Fair fishing can be had in most years, early in the season, for planted rainbow trout 9 to 11 inches. Facilities include a small boat launch and only limited parking. Located 3 miles north of Tenino.

Lake St. Clair - A few rainbow trout and bass are available all year at St. Clair, along with kokanee in the summer months. Located 5 miles southeast of Lacey.

Summit Lake - Fair fishing for small rainbows early in the season here. Cutthroat trout, kokanee and bass inhabit Summit as well. Also known as Prays Lake as far back as 1860. Some handicapped facilities and a state boat launch.

WALLA WALLA COUNTY

Virgil B. Bennington Lake - Formerly Mill Creek Reservoir, built by the USA Corps of Engineers in the 1940's. Receives a large planting of catchable-size rainbow trout annually, when water levels allow. Good bank fishing access and boat ramp.

WHATCOM COUNTY

Baker Lake - This large reservoir, 6 miles northeast of Concrete offers good kokanee fishing in May and June. Kokanee fishing picks up again in the fall. Known as an excellent producer of rainbow trout in July also. Check the current regulations or call the WDFW office for the most up to date slot or size limits. A boat launch and public access are available.

Cain Lake - Often seen as Woodmere or Windemere Lake on early maps, Cain is located 10 miles southeast of Bellingham off I-5 near the Alger exit. The 72 acre lake is surrounded by summer homes and permanent residences, but still provides fair trout and bass fishing.

Diablo Lake - Located in the Ross Lake National Recreation Area, 6 miles northeast of Newhalem. Fishing can be steady, at times, for rainbow trout. The Thunder Arm is a good bet for fly fishing from a small boat. Boat launching facilities as well as campgrounds are available.

Fazon Lake - This 32 acre lake, off the Hemmi road, has a small boat launch that can be crowded at times. Fazon, which lies in a peat bog area, is a mixed species lake containing rainbow and cutthroat trout, largemouth bass, bluegill, and catfish. Check current regulations for slot and size limits on bass, as well as possession limit on catfish. Some handicapped facilities. Good summer bluegill fishing.

Galena Chain Lakes - A group of four lakes on the northwest side of Table Mountain, about 2 miles from Mt. Baker Lodge. Arbuthnot, Hayes, Mazama, and Iceberg contain small eastern brook trout. Expect a pleasant hike-in after the trail is open (usually in August).

Gorge Lake - Located 3 miles northeast of Newhalem, Gorge contains rainbow and cutthroat trout.

Lake Padden - Located along Samish Way in a Bellingham City Park, Padden is a popular spot for locals to jog, picnic and fish. Fishing for stocked rainbow trout is usually very good opening week. Fly fishing improves in May and June, when some big cutthroat are taken on mayfly imitations. Kokanee can be plentiful in some years. No gasoline motors allowed.

Ross Lake - This huge Seattle City Light reservoir has a boat launch at the north end accessible through British Columbia. The Ross Lake Resort provides transportation or boat rentals on the U.S. side. (206) 386-4437. The trout in Ross are believed to be steelhead that were landlocked when the Skagit River was dammed in the 1930's. Fishing for these native rainbows is open for a limited short, late season and regulations should be carefully checked each year for new catch, size or slot limits. Regulations are strictly enforced here because the fishery was nearly depleted to the point of no return. Quick action by the regional fish biologist helped implement conservation measures just in time.

Lake Samish - The best fishing is in June and September for the kokanee that inhabit Samish. Located off I-5, 6 miles south of Bellingham, the lake also contains bass, perch and some cutthroat trout. A boat launch and park are available.

Silver Lake - This 173 acre lake is located 3 miles north of Maple Fall off the Mt. Baker Highway. Stocked with rainbow trout for opening week, it also contains bigger cutthroat. Silver is very crowded on opening day, but has good shore fishing areas and a boat launch in the county park. Called "Fish Lake" years ago.

Squalicum Lake - A fly fishing-only lake with walk-in access from the Mt. Baker Highway. Contains small cutthroat trout.

Terrell Lake - This 438 acre lake is known for it's spiny ray fishing, but does contain a few cutthroat trout. Located 5 miles west of Ferndale. Check current regulations for slot and size limits on bass. A Fishing dock extends from the west shore, and a boat ramp is available. A good place to watch water fowl, especially the beautiful trumpeter swan.

Toad Lake - Called "Emerald Lake" by local real estate agents, this 29 acre lake is located 5 miles northeast of Bellingham off Britton Road. A popular opening day destination, Toad can be

Twin Lakes near Mt. Baker in Whatcom County.

excellent for stocked rainbow trout. Some kokanee are also available.

Twin Lakes - Located in the Swamp Creek drainage near Winchester Mountain, these high lakes offer fishing for small eastern brook trout. Very rough, steep road not accessible until July. Check for road closure, may be hike-in some years.

Lake Whatcom - A large, natural lake stabilized by a dam, it contains cutthroat trout, kokanee and bass. The area between Electric Avenue Bridge and the outlet dam is closed to all fishing (protected spawning habitat). Always check current regulations because these rules are strictly enforced. A nice boat launch is available at Bloedel-Donovan Park.

Wiser Lake - This 123 acre lake is located 3 miles southwest of Lynden off the Guide Meridian. It is a mixed species lake containing a few cutthroat and spiny rays. Boat ramp east of the Guide.

WHITMAN COUNTY

Klemgaard Park Pond - This waterway, in the county park outside Colfax, gets rainbow trout plants each year.

Pampa Pond - Rainbow trout are planted each year in this 3 acre pond, located 4 miles west of LaCross. Bank fishing only is available, but average catch reports can be exceptionally good on opening day here. Look for early closure date.

Riparian Pond - Located just below Little Goose Dam off the Snake River. This small pond is planted with nice rainbow trout catchables in the spring each year. Any that carry-over to late summer and fall grow even bigger.

Rock Lake - Rock is the largest natural lake in Southeast

Washington. It is about 7 miles long and bordered almost the entire length by basalt cliffs on both sides. Located 1 mile north of Highway 23 and the town of Ewan, Rock contains some fair-size brown and rainbow trout established from fry plants. As a side note; nice largemouth bass are available in summer months. A boat launch exists on the south end.

YAKIMA COUNTY

Bear Lake - A small lake in the Oak Creek Wildlife Area, about 15 miles west of Naches. Planted each year with catchable and fingerling rainbow trout, it is usually not accessible by vehicle until May. The Wildlife Area provides prime elk habitat.

Bumping Reservoir - A good kokanee fishery exists here, and all methods are productive including trolling, still and fly fishing. Fish run small, 6 to 9 inches. Best fishing starts in mid-May. Some 8 to 11 inch rainbows also. Excellent public campgrounds and a boat ramp are available.

Dog Lake - This 61 acre lake lies east of White Pass along Highway 12. It is at an elevation of 4207 feet, so it doesn't start to yield results until early June. Fishing is good for 7 to 10 inch rainbow and brook trout. A large Forest Service campground and rough boat launch are adjacent to the lake.

Leech Lake - A 41 acre fly fishing-only lake situated at a high elevation of 4412 feet. Leech offers fine fly fishing for 8 to 14 inch brook trout in the summer months. Facilities include a Forest Service campground and boat launch. Leech lies just east of White Pass and is usually ice-free by early June. Check special regulations for catch and size limits.

Wenas Lake - One of the best known brown trout fisheries in Central Washington, Wenas also produces many 8 to 12 inch rainbows. Check special regulations regarding limits on brown trout.

FLY FISHING
Tackle for Washington Lakes

RODS

The fly rod is of primary importance when lake fishing in the pacific northwest. Not only must the rod be versatile for casting distance and accuracy, it needs to be durable so that it will last for many seasons in the wet, damp conditions of this region. During the early years of Washington fly fishing, anglers plied the lakes with split bamboo rods made by the classic western rod builders E.C. Powell, Lew Stoner (Winston), and Bill Phillipson. Although a few of these rods are still fished today, most have been retired to a display case.

Rod manufacturers focused their attention on tubular fiberglass technology during the 1960's. Fiberglass rods were lighter, cheaper, and stronger than bamboo rods of comparable size. In the 1970's, carbon fiber (graphite) was developed as an aerospace material, and was soon adapted as a component for fishing rod blanks. After a few years graphite replaced fiberglass as the favored fly rod material. Today, northwest anglers can select from literally hundreds of designs. Some of the most popular graphite fly rods used in Washington are made by Winston, Orvis, St. Croix, Lamiglas, G. Loomis, and Bainbridge Island's own Sage Rod Company.

Graphite is near perfect as a fly rod material. Graphite fly rods are very light (and keep getting lighter - almost to a fault!) , virtually indestructible, and extremely sensitive to the strike of a fish. Unfortunately, as rods get better and more refined, prices seem to go even higher. If you are on a budget and cannot afford to buy three or four different rods for all line weights functional in trout fishing, consider my ideal, all around trout fly rod and follow these steps to it's purchase:

(1) Buy a good quality, brand name rod. You do not necessarily have to buy the maker's top of the line series. Most rod companies market a line of rods for "beginners". Some of these so-called beginner rods are simply great fly rods, with quality blanks, less expensive hardware, and a cheaper case. These are often constructed with blanks having softer, "parabolic" actions that a surprising number of experienced anglers prefer.

(2) Select a long rod of at least 9 feet. For most lake fishing, where the angler sits low in a boat or float tube, a longer rod of 9 1/2 feet is very advantageous in casting and maneuvering the fly line. Washington is a land of open water and windy conditions. This is no place for seven foot midge rods, unless you want a challenge and perhaps a hook in your ear from the backcast!

(3) Decide on either a 5 or 6 weight line rating. Many rods are rated as a 5/6, which usually means they are a bit heavier than a true 5 weight. I like a 5 weight because I enjoy casting to rising fish on fairly calm water, and the 5 makes for a more delicate presentation. A 6 weight line will cut through the wind better than the 5 and the rod will have more power for longer casts and bigger fish. A long, 6 weight fly rod can also fill-in for light bass or sea run cutthroat fishing because the line weight will handle moderately dressed size 8 and 10 streamers.

One popular option is to build a fly rod from a kit. Some fly and tackle shops offer packaged kits or will sell the rod blank and give the angler several reel seat and cork choices. Rod kits, blanks, and components, along with instruction books, are available from fly tackle mail order houses as well.

REELS

Fly reels must have a sensitive drag to protect thin tippet material from breaking under the strain of a large trout. It is difficult enough to catch an 18 inch plus fish, so why have the handicap of a jerky, rough reel. For years, the most popular fly reel used in Washington was the Pflueger Medalist. Some of the old, made in U.S.A. Medalists are still functional today, and a modern version remains in production. Another classic is the English made Hardy Perfect, considered by many, in the northwest, to be the finest fly reel ever made. Advanced manufacturing technology now provides the angler with a number of good reels from which to choose.

In selecting a single action fly reel for trout fishing in lakes, consider the following factors: (1) Weight of the reel so that it balances well with the fly rod you intend to use. (2) Size and line capacity of the reel. It must be able to hold at least 50 yards of #20 backing, along with the fly line. Remember that a double taper line, due to the nature of the design, takes up more space on the reel spool and requires added capacity. To be safe, buy a reel that is 3 inches in diameter or larger. (3) Smooth drag operation ... or delicate click in a reel with no drag. (4) Durability and simplicity of construction because the reel will definitely get wet and dirty. For this reason, an automatic fly reel is not recommended.

If price is not a consideration, buy one of the superb, machined aluminum reels from Orvis, Sage, Hardy, Ross, or one of the Lamson reels (made in Washington). Orvis, Daiwa, Martin, Cortland, and Scientific Anglers make fine, economically priced single action fly reels that might better fit your budget. At least, try to invest in one good reel, with available extra spools to hold a sinking line.

FLY LINE

There are essentially two major manufacturers of quality fly lines today; Cortland and Scientific Anglers. Both market several premium lines offering the most advanced technology available. If you can possibly afford one of these, it is a worthy investment. I have a Scientific Anglers "Ultra" line going on seven years old, that has been fished hard and has not yet cracked or deteriorated. If price is a factor, both of these companies sell "budget" fly lines that are more than adequate for most conditions. Several specialty lines have also been developed bearing the name of known anglers and these certainly warrant a look, for specific applications.

In any case, if you can own only <u>one</u> fly line for trout fishing in lakes, buy a top quality weight-forward floating line (in 5 or 6 weight depending upon the rod). A double-taper floating line might be your preference if you like to execute optimum roll-casts and desire a slightly more delicate taper ... but it will not shoot a cast as far. The floating line will suffice for almost all lake fishing in the State of Washington. Dry flies, emergers, nymphs, streamers, and even *chironomids* can be successfully presented with the floating line!

Quite a few seasoned Washington fly fishers attack a lake with only the floating line. A long leader and weighted fly, make the presentation to the bottom when fish are deep. Of course, there are many sinking lines available that get the job done quicker, and most people carry an extra reel or spool filled with some type of sinking fly line.

A vast selection of "sink-tip" fly lines can be made or purchased with a 10 to 30 foot weighted tip section attached to a floating, running line. The floating portion can act as a strike indicator. Alternative lines such as these are intriguing, but not essential in Washington lake fishing. Should you decide to procure a sink-tip line for fishing below the surface, a <u>medium</u> sink rate is recommended. The medium sink rate will get you there quick enough and be smoother to cast than the latest "super fast" sink-tips (which tend to hinge and need to be lofted rather than cast). Often, the super- fast sink lines will snag the bottom in still water, especially when fishing near shoreline structure.

If you like to troll or "mooch" a fly from a small boat, canoe, or float tube, purchase a conventional medium sinking line. A medium or moderate sink rate will put the fly below the surface at a slow trolling speed, without dragging on the bottom. Fly fishermen that are self-propelled in a float tube have an added advantage because they can more easily vary their speed to cover different levels or come to a complete stop to let the fly sink deeper. Sitting right in the water, from a float tube, it is

Some of the author's nymph and pupa imitations present a "buggy" silhouette.

sometimes possible to see structure or feeding trout near the bottom. With a medium sinking line the angler can maneuver the fly to the correct depth by moving along more slowly or lifting and lowering the rod.

LEADERS AND TIPPETS

The strategic link between the fly line and fly is the leader. Commercially prepared, knotless, tapered leaders are the best way to go, unless you enjoy tying blood knots and straining your eyes! Knotted leaders tend to pick up moss, or lake vegetation, causing more problems than they are worth. Commercial leaders are designed by computers to turn-over well when matched with an appropriate size fly. Generally, select a leader with a tippet rating from 4X (approximately 6lb.) down to 7X (approximately 2lb.).

The size of the fly, more importantly than the anticipated weight of the fish, tends to determine which tippet is used. A small, size 16 or 18 fly will require a maximum 6X or 7X tippet diameter for good presentation. If the tippet material is too heavy, the fly will not sit well in the water nor will the material fit through the hook eye! Conversely, if a long, light tippet is tied to a heavy size 6 streamer or leech pattern...the leader will "hinge" and not turn-over properly.

For most lake fishing in Washington, a 9 foot leader is used with a tippet rating of 5X or 6X. This will accommodate dry flies, soft hackles, nymphs and chironomids from size 10 - 16. A shorter, 4 -7 foot leader with a tippet rating of approximately 4X may be necessary for streamers, dragon fly nymphs, and leeches.

When your leader breaks, it is most economical to tie on a new tippet section with a blood knot, rather than replace the whole leader. Buy spools of extra tippet material in 7X,6X,5X and 4X. These can be added to lengthen an existing leader, or combined to make special variations.

COMMERCIALLY TIED FLIES

Even the most expert fly tyer will, on occasion, buy a commercially tied fly to copy or fish. Not all flies sold in Washington are made in Washington. Imported flies from other States and the Orient are the norm in both fly fishing shops and sporting goods stores. Most are excellent flies, tied on high quality hooks with top grade materials. Some local Washington and northwest regional patterns are now available from imported sources. However, many good shops will carry locally tied flies that work well here, in a color, size or shape that better imitates the insects of specific Washington lakes. Northwest *chironomid* larva, especially the blood worm, are usually best if found locally tied. *Callibaetis* emergers, and damsel fly nymphs are other examples of Washington lake patterns that I have found to be better if tied locally. Also, "tied in shop" flies are often rendered barbless for releasing fish.

If you are in doubt as to the quality of a fly, or it's likeness to an insect you wish to imitate, do not hesitate to ask the opinion of a knowledgeable friend or fly fishing shop clerk. Moreover, don't underestimate your own sense of judgment. Make sure the hook is sharp, the eye is clear, and that the fly looks "buggy". On a dry fly, inspect the hackles...they should be stiff, and not webby or soft. Toss the dry up into the air. It should land softly in your hand, level, with the hook down. When buying nymphs, check the dubbing to see if it is secure to the hook shank, by slightly twisting the body of the fly. If it is too loose, the fly won't last for many fish!

ACCESSORIES

While it is possible to fish from the shore of some Washington lakes, most anglers rely on a floating platform such as a boat, canoe, or float tube. As private property rights have taken away public shore access to many lakes, a boat or tube is fast becoming a necessity.

Float tubes ("belly boats") have developed nicely since the days of simple, glorified inner tubes. Two of the better selling float tubes in Washington are the Oregon made Caddis and those of Bucks Bags. The traditional donut style float tube that has to be stepped into, is the most economical design in terms of price and space. A commercial truck inner tube is sheathed in durable cordura nylon material, which is sewn to give the tube a more oblong shape when inflated within. A high back support with a separate inflatable bladder is best, unless you want to conserve weight (backpacking models come with no back support). Better float tubes are equipped with zippered compartments for holding a camera, food, jacket or extra gear. Easy entry float tube models are also available in a horseshoe shape. The latest, and most expensive product to hit the market is a small, personal platform boat.

Chest Waders are essential in float tubing a cold water fishery. Neoprene material waders are best, although it is possible to fish in lightweight nylon waders during the summer months. Buy the best you can afford.

A good pair of float tube fins are needed to propel yourself through the water, especially when maneuvering to cast in the direction of a rising trout. I strap the fins right over my wading boots for added ankle support. The weight of the boots is almost completely displaced when submerged in the lake. If you suffer from leg fatigue, tie a couple of ping-pong paddles to your tube. When your feet get tired, use these like a set of miniature oars (I learned this trick from an innovative one-legged fly fisherman!). Remember not to cover more distance in the tube than you can comfortably handle on the return trip. On windy days, be careful, you may get blown down-lake and have to hike back to your original launch area.

The float tube is a fun, effective tool for lake fishing. Being almost eye to eye with the trout, and literally swimming in the water yourself is one of the most intimate of all angling experiences.

"Mooching" a fly from a float tube produced this 21-inch rainbow trout for the author.

FLY FISHING
Techniques for Washington Lakes

MOOCHING A FLY

Perhaps the easiest, and one of the most productive of all fly fishing techniques is trolling or "mooching" a fly. In fact, many northwest anglers are first introduced to fly fishing through this method. Since no casting is required, it is an ideal way for beginners or kids to be able to fish at one of the special "fly fishing only" lakes. Furthermore, experienced fly fishers will sometimes mooch or drift a fly in order to cover a larger area at an unfamiliar lake, or when there is no apparent insect hatch during the late season.

The "mooching method" is simple. Utilizing a slightly weighted, attractor fly and a 5 to 7 foot tapered leader, strip off 20 to 30 feet of floating fly line and let it drift behind the boat or float tube. If a sinking line is used, shorten the leader to 4 feet. I like the floating line for most situations where trout are feeding just below the surface on emerging insects (often in the spring during early morning and evening). Row, paddle or fin at a very slow speed, or just drift. Lift the rod tip slowly from time to time so the fly will move toward the surface.

Proper fly selection for mooching is important, but there are a good variety of searching patterns that have proven to be successful over the years. This makes life easier for the novice, because no experience is required to imitate a particular insect hatch. For most trout and even kokanee, the angler can fish a basic soft hackle wet fly in size 10 to 14. True soft hackle trout flies are tied with a sparse body, no tail, and partridge, grouse, or hen hackle. Purchase or tie these in olive, gray and brown to roughly imitate most mayflies, caddis and the smaller damsel flies that inhabit Washington lakes.

The classic northwest attractor pattern is the Carey Special. If you plan to mooch or drift a fly on Washington lakes, the Carey can be your most valuable tool. It was originated by British Columbia's Colonel Carey, prior to 1930. The use of long, soft pheasant rump hackles that extend back beyond the hook bend, sets the Carey apart from other patterns of that period in trout fishing history. Although it was intended to imitate an emerging sedge (caddis) near the lake surface, the Carey can be fished deep on a sinking line, as a dragon fly nymph. Actually, the versatile Carey can be trolled or mooched at any depth to meet the conditions of the day.

Anglers are not limited to the colors of those early Carey Specials, tied with brown bodies and natural pheasant. Pheasant rump hackles are now available in dyed colors, and the body can be dubbed or wound of most materials, including wool, rabbit, squirrel, or synthetics. A rib of tinsel makes the Carey into a flashier streamer. Add Marabou to the wing for additional movement in the water. If you do not make your own flies, many variations of the Carey can be purchased at local Washington fly shops.

Leech patterns are another series of mooching flies that are well suited for Washington lakes. One widely available design of this type is the rabbit-fur leech. A long-shanked hook is prepared with a shaggy wool (or similar material) body that is brushed or combed back. A "wing" made of a slender rabbit fur strip is tied to the top of the hook, along the shank, extending just past the bend. As the fly moves through the water, the fine rabbit fur undulates back and forth. For this reason, rabbit leeches can also be cast and retrieved-in toward the boat or float tube.

The famous Woolly-Bugger fly is well known as a leech-type attractor pattern. This design has all the characteristics of a good searching fly and displays fluid movement in the water. It is tied simply with a long marabou tail and palmered hackle over a chenille body. The key to a good Woolly-Bugger or similar Woolly Worm, is the use of soft, webby hackles tied wet fly style (slanting backward from the hook eye). If the hackles used are too stiff and short or tied-in the wrong way, the fly will not show as much movement, especially when slow mooching or drifting.

If you like to fish at night, particularly on the Washington desert lakes, mooching a leech pattern from a float tube can produce large trout. In the dark when it becomes more difficult to cast, tie on a black, brown or purple leech imitation. Proceed at a slow, relaxed pace letting the fly sink to various depths. Every so often, retrieve some line or lift the rod tip slightly. Experiment with different speeds and retrieves until you meet with success.

A discussion on trolling a fly cannot end without mentioning the Doc Spratley. This old Canadian pattern is a compact streamer that sinks quickly and serves well as a fry imitation at intermediate depths. Buy or tie a few Spratleys in black, brown, and dark olive. Try it when all else fails.

CHIRONOMID FISHING

Chironomids are part of the large Diptera order of true flies. During the spring and early summer, the small chironomid pupae slowly ascend to the surface of Washington lakes. Trout feed on this insect at various depths, from just above the muddy bottom to within the surface film. As the chironomids wiggle slowly upward, trout pick them off in big numbers.

In what has become a northwest tradition each year, fly fishers first pursue trout with chironomid patterns fished near the bottom in April and May. The method used is reminiscent of still-fishing with a bobber or cork float. It is as follows: (1) Depending on the depth (usually 12 to 16 feet), a very long leader of corresponding size is attached to the end of the fly line. (2) Before tying on the fly, slide a small "corkie" (strike indicator) up to near the butt of the leader and secure it with a piece of

Small cutthroat rise to emerging insects on Squalicum Lake.

toothpick. (3) Tie on a weighted chironomid pattern in maroon, brown or black. (4) loft the whole "rig" a few yards from the boat or float tube and let the fly sink to the bottom. (5) Lift the rod tip every 30 seconds and watch the strike indicator.

Chironomids can also be fished on the bottom with a sinking line and a short leader, for those anglers who prefer to fish by "feel" rather than "sight".

Dead drifting at various depths or fishing a chironomid pattern near the surface are two other effective techniques for spring and early summer trout fishing. Look for the presence of chironomid casings on the waters surface. These can often be spotted just as they are shed by the adult, which looks like a small mosquito. When this type of insect activity is taking place, cast and retrieve or slowly drift an unweighted chironomid pattern over the area. The intent is to imitate the pupa just before it reaches the surface film. Once the natural reaches the surface, it sheds the pupal shuck, becomes a winged adult and is of less interest to the trout.

With word out on the success of chironomid fishing, most shops now sell at least a few basic imitations such as the blood worm (red chironomid larva), or the venerable TDC (a Canadian pattern). Tie or purchase chironomid imitations in fundamental natural colors such as brown, black, or maroon in sizes 10 - 16, with some weighted for bottom fishing.

MATCHING THE SPRING CALLIBAETIS HATCH

A most prolific hatch of insects that occurs on Washington lakes, in the spring, is that of the *Callibaetis* mayfly. Less significant, yet productive hatches and spinners (spent females) can also be observed in summer and fall. The Callibaetis is a small, gray, speckled-wing mayfly having a delicate, thin body. Most anglers would agree that it is the predominant mayfly on Washington still waters.

Traditionally, the adult (winged version) is imitated with the Adams dry fly in size 12 to 16. The original Adams is actually an east coast pattern. Specific variations have been developed for several northwest lakes, such as the Chopaka May, for use on the lake of the same name. It is true that many Washington fly fishermen still utilize some form of the Adams for their Callibaetis patterns combining "grizzly" (variegated) cock hackle, with a quill or lightly dubbed gray body. However, a progressive trend in the northwest, is the use of emerger flies that imitate the nymph in it's transitional phase.

Emerger fishing is rapidly becoming "the hot, new way" to present a fly on northwest lakes. The most important reason for the methods success lies in the fact that big trout feed more heavily on emerging nymphs before they mature into the adult (winged phase of the mayfly life cycle).

The finest pattern for imitating the emerging Callibaetis, or any mayfly for that matter, is the soft hackle fly. A simple, but effective Callibaetis soft hackle can be tied on any wet fly hook using a sparse wing of gray partridge or hen over a body of gray rabbit or mole fur. Size 14 seems to match the insect under most conditions.

If you see slurping or "bulging" trout finning just below the surface, they are probably feeding on emergers. Even a light swirl on the surface or a dimple on the water can indicate a big fish slowly feeding. The best strategy is to cast quickly, presenting the fly within one or two feet of the rise. It is preferable to "lead" the fish by placing the fly in its path, and twitching or retrieving it a bit. If you can get the fly to the area of the rise before 3 to 5 seconds have elapsed, chances are the fish will return and you will be hooked-up. This type of sight fishing is very challenging and requires accurate casts and quick reflexes. When trout are rising to Callibaetis in all directions, emerger fishing can get pretty exciting!

Of course, a dry fly can also be productive in this situation, but I prefer the soft hackle fly for several reasons: (1) The soft hackle has better movement in the water and consequently produces more strikes when only a few insects are hatching. The trout are attracted by the movement. (2) The soft hackle fly sits in the water not on the water like a buoyant, dry fly. Trout tend to bump or push over a dry fly, and because of this buoyancy, some strikes are missed. The soft hackle lies firmly in the water, is not pushed around by the fish, and produces a better hook-up to strike success ratio. (3) Presentation and casting of soft hackle and emerger flies is less complicated (4) And for those of us who are not so nimble, soft hackles are easier to tie than delicate dry flies.

Always remember to use the lightest tippet material possible when fishing soft hackle flies. A heavy leader and tippet can impede the movement of the fly and it will not appear natural to the trout. If you use a light tippet, a few fish will probably break-off, but you will be rewarded with twice the action!

DAMSELS AND DRAGONS

No fairy tale here. When the water begins to warm in the summer, damsel and dragon fly nymphs become an important trout food on Washington lakes. The damsel nymph is of primary interest to fly fishermen in late May, June and July. At that time, these wiggly members of the *Odonata* order can be observed swimming erratically in the shallow water of many northwest lakes.

Some of the best damsel fly nymph imitations incorporate marabou in the tail or beard. A body can be formed from rabbit dubbing, followed by a wing case pulled over a set of monofilament eyes. Almost without exception, damsel nymphs are a shade of green or olive. Commercially tied damsels can be quite elaborate, yet a simple impressionistic version without eyes or a wing case will produce good results. Buy or tie these in size 8-10 (or smaller for late summer). A small damsel nymph pattern (size 12 or 14) can also sufficiently imitate the fresh water shrimp or "scuds" found in alkali content lakes. Sometimes damsels are tied on a bent hook to impart a squirming action to the fly. This action can also be brought about by twitching the rod tip during the retrieve.

Though it has been disregarded by most anglers, the adult damsel imitation can be effective in the late summer and fall. Better tie up a few for yourself because not many of the blue flies are made commercially.

The dragon fly nymph, a big cousin to the damsel, is an active lake dweller that provides food for large trout. Fish these bulky flies down, near the bottom or through lake vegetation with a short leader. It may be necessary to use a heavier rod and line (#7-8) if you intend to cast dragon fly nymph imitations very far. Some species of dragon nymphs move sporadically and prey on other insects with quick bursts of speed. Therefore it is advantageous to retrieve the imitation in a like manner.

16" rainbow about to be released, was enticed by a damsel nymph.

CADDIS FLIES

Numerous forms and quantities of caddis flies are found in Washington lakes. The adult caddis can be distinguished by a down wing that covers the body in a moth-like appearance. It is commonly called "sedge" in Canada. In fact, the Lake Sedge or so-called Traveling Sedge hatch is a popular emergence to fish, in July, on the Kamloops area lakes of British Columbia.

Summer and fall marks the time of greatest abundance for caddis flies in Washington. Perceptive fishermen will want to observe the insects activity. The pupae swim quickly and steadily in their ascent to the lake surface. Just before reaching the surface film, where they transform into the adult, caddis pupa are extremely vulnerable to feeding trout. Soft hackle flies in brown, tan, and beige work very well to imitate these emergers. Actually, another good fly is the old standard Gold Ribbed Hare's Ear. Keep a variety of sizes on hand because proportion, rather than exact color, seems to be the factor that determines success. When presenting a caddis imitation, let it sink and then retrieve with a long, even lift of the rod.

During warm evenings on Washington lakes, the swarms of caddis adults can be so thick that spectacled anglers find it necessary to brush them away from their eyeglasses! If you enjoy fishing adult caddis imitations, right on the surface, a great fly pattern to try is the Tom Thumb. Traditional Tom Thumbs are constructed entirely of hollow, natural or brown deer hair and consequently float like a cork. Commercially tied Tom Thumbs may be hard to find so, in the alternative, the equally effective Elk Hair Caddis or Humpy can be purchased.

Casting a dry fly at Merry Lake.

OTHER METHODS
Progressive Techniques for the Non Fly-Fisher

Many trout anglers in Washington State do not fly fish or do so only on occasion. Spinning (and spin casting) tackle is widely used on most Washington lakes. However, it is illegal to fish with spinning tackle on lakes designated "fly fishing only" (even if the lure is a "fly"). These lakes happen to be among the best producers of large trout in the State; so learning to use a fly rod would be a logical step for a spin angler seeking to catch more trophy fish.

For those anglers not inclined to pick up a fly rod, kids, non-angler parents, and ultra-light spin aficionados; we offer the following tips and interesting methods that may be helpful!

THOUGHTS ON TACKLE

Certainly, there is a magnitude of spinning gear on the market. It is unfortunate that so many short, stiff graphite spinning rods are sold today. A little more length, softness, and better components would improve the quality and appeal of these rods immensely. Recently, some manufacturers have begun marketing "classic" fiberglass spinning rods that are reasonably priced and reminiscent of the great *S-Glass, Conolon,* and *Silaflex* rods of the 1960's.

For accurate casts of weighted flies and ultra-light lures, try using a moderate action, light spinning rod of 6 - 7 1/2 feet or more. The longer rod is better for float tubing, and keeps the line away from the boat when trolling. One option is to make, or have custom made, an ultra-light spinning rod on a fly rod blank. Just be sure it is constructed with plenty of guides. The old "foul proof" style guides are superior for moderate action blanks because they flex with the rod (but, these are hard to find). Fugi single foot guides are also excellent. An all-cork handle, with rings or a quality reel seat, is very comfortable.

Dozens of spinning reels are displayed in sporting goods and department stores everywhere. Beginning in the 1980's, skirted spool spinning reels appeared on the tackle scene and the design endured. Graphite is now incorporated in the construction of many reels and has the advantage of being very light. However, lightness and fancy trimmings are not the most valuable features in a spinning reel. Without question, a smooth drag, with a sensitive range of settings, is the most important criteria for selecting a spinning reel. Smooth line movement from the spool through the bail is imperative when using 2 and 4 lb. test! And, of course, light line means better lure action, less visibility in the water, and more fish.

FISHING A FLY WITH SPINNING TACKLE

When I caught my first trout on a fly, I was not using a fly rod. As a teenager, with no fly fishing uncles to teach me the skill of the long rod, I improvised by attaching a cork float to my ultralight spinning outfit; splicing on a 4 foot leader and a dry fly (purchased at the local drug store). With this rig, I took rainbow trout in mountain creeks and brook trout in alpine lakes that would at times refuse other offerings such as bait or lures. Soon thereafter, my friends and I discovered small, clear "bubbles" that were specially made just for this technique. They could also be filled with a bit of water to lengthen our casts.

What we thought was our innovation, had actually been around for years. Eugene Burns in his book, Advanced Fly Fishing, discussed the use of a float to cast a dry fly with spinning gear back in the 1950's. For whatever reason, this effective method is still disregarded by most spin fishermen. If you do not own a fly rod and want to make your spinning gear more versatile, try fishing a dry fly or soft hackle with a light leader and bubble. Don't miss out on the opportunity to pursue trout with an imitation of their favorite food...aquatic insects.

The weighted trout fly is generally overlooked as a "lure" for spinning. Many larger, heavily weighted patterns such as the Hare's Ear, Doc Sprately, and leech designs, like the Woolly Worm, can be adequately cast with ultra-light spinning gear, some split shot, and 2 to 4 lb. test line. Even small, weighted chironomid larva imitations can be sunk to the bottom and manipulated with ultra-light spinning gear. And, trolling with a weighted leech pattern or streamer is easy with spinning equipment.

Spin fishermen who go out in a float tube can mooch a weighted fly as previously described. With a tube, it is possible to maneuver in-close to the area of feeding trout. Quiet and stealth can accomplish this. Again, remember to check for tackle restrictions. A true fly rod, reel and line is required on "fly fishing only" lakes. Special regulations on other lakes may demand a single-barbless hook for flies or lures.

OPENING DAY STRATEGIES

Near the end of April, most lakes in Washington open for trout fishing. The best "strategy", if you don't like crowds, is to stay home! Shorelines, boat ramps and parking areas are full of all sorts of folks itching to catch their limit and capture bragging rights for the quickest stringer or biggest broodstocker. The good thing about opening day at one of the more popular spots is...there are tons of trout. This is the perfect time to bring small children because the potential for success is great, and the chance of disappointment is minimal.

Most fisher people are friendly, but when things get crowded and tempers are edgy remember that fishing for stocked rainbows can be almost as good the <u>day after opening day</u>. I always take my kids out the next day after school and we do fine.

Although stocked trout are usually plentiful, the following proven technique will enhance anyone's ability to catch more fish with bait on opening day or in the next few weeks after: (1) Use a 2 lb. test leader (or less) of about 2-3 feet long, attached to a tiny swivel with no snap. (2) Before knotting the main line to the other end of the swivel, slip it through the middle of a small egg shaped sinker. (3) Next, knot the main line to the swivel, allowing the sinker to slide freely between the rod and that end of the swivel. (4) Use your favorite bait of salmon eggs, nightcrawlers, or uggh...garlic cheese. Place it on a size 12, 14 or 16 hook of appropriate style, so that it completely covers the hook. For an even bigger advantage, use one of the wonderful chemically sharpened hooks or re-sharpen a standard hook yourself.

There is a sound principle behind the sliding sinker rig. When a trout nibbles (mouths) the bait, it will feel no resistance from the sinker. The sinker sits on the bottom as the line runs freely through it. Be sure to leave some slack in your line to allow the trout to pick up the bait and move off. When the line goes tight, wait a few seconds and then set the hook!

The single most important tip I can give for opening day or early season bait fishing is; use a light, small diameter leader. Trout will pass right by the guy next to you using 10 pound test and feed on your rig with 1 or 2 pound test. Heavy line spooks fish and restricts the movement of flies, lures or bait. At times I have used 7X fly fishing tippet material of very fine diameter to help my kids get fish when things were slow opening day and trout were picky. So, go light and sneaky for more fish.

If you cast or troll a lure on opening day, run it low and slow. The best retrieve is sometimes as slow as you can turn the handle of your reel, right along the bottom at drop-offs or ledges parallel to the shore.

And what about mid-May and June when it seems like all the trout are gone or the lake is "fished out"? A good guess would be that a large majority of the stocked trout have been caught, and those that remain have acclimated to the lake environment and are feeding on aquatic insects. It is a time to begin fly fishing or start thinking about bass!

Large trout, like this 22-inch rainbow, are often found in Washington's desert lakes.

CAREY SPECIAL

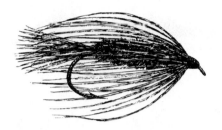

Hook: Mustad 9672 or equivalent ~ Size 6, 8, and 10
Tail: Pheasant rump hackle fibers (natural)
Body: Olive, brown, or black chenille; or mohair yarn
Hackle: Long pheasant rump feather (color can be varied)

DOC SPRATLEY

Hook: Mustad 9672 or equivalent ~ Size 6, 8, and 10
Tail: Guinea hackle fibers
Body: Olive, black or brown wool yarn
Rib: Fine silver tinsel
Wing: Pheasant tail fibers
Throat: Guinea hackle fibers
Head: Wound peacock herl

CHIRONOMID PUPA

Hook: Mustad 9671 ~ Size 10, 12, 14, and 16
Body: Black, brown, green, or maroon floss
Rib: White floss or thread
Wing Case: Dyed brown turkey
Thorax: Black or brown rabbit fur dubbing
Head Area: White ostrich over-wrapped with black thread

BLOOD WORM

Hook: Mustad 9671 or equivalent ~ Size 12, 14, and 16
Body: Soft (not coarse) wool yarn dyed claret or deep red
Rib: Fine copper wire
Head Area: Wine color rabbit fur dubbing
Optional: A few wraps of narrow-gauge lead wire

ADAMS
(Callibaetis Mayfly)

Hook: Mustad 94840 or equivalent ~ Size 12, 14, and 16
Tail: Moose body hair
Body: Light gray or dun rabbit fur dubbing
Wing: "Grizzly", paired hackle tips
Hackle: Dun or brown

SOFT HACKLE ATTRACTOR
(Emerger)

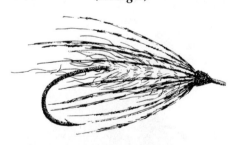

Hook: Mustad 94840 (dry fly) or a light wet fly hook #12 to 16
Body: Gray rabbit dubbing or mole fur (Callibaetis emerger)
Hackle: Partridge, grouse, or domestic hen
Head: Black silk or 8/0 thread
Note: For caddis emerger use body shades of brown

TOM THUMB
(Adult Caddis)

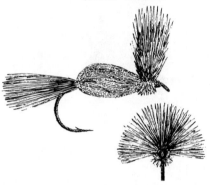

Hook: Mustad 94840 or equivalent ~ Size10, 12, and 14
Tail: Stacked deer hair with tips back
Body and Wing: One clump of deer body hair, tied in at base of tail and pulled forward with a twist.

ELK HAIR CADDIS
(Dry Fly)

Hook: Mustad 94840 or equivalent dry fly hook #10 to 16
Body: Rabbit fur dubbing dyed brown, orange or yellow
Hackle: Brown, palmered
Wing: Elk hair, natural or brown, slanted back 45 degrees
Head: Elk hair clipped after wing is tied in

RABBIT-FUR LEECH

Hook: Mustad 79580 or equivalent ~ Size 6, 8, and 10
Body: Wool or mohair yarn dyed black, brown or dark olive
Wing: Prepared rabbit fur strip tied in "zonker style"
Wing Color: Match body

WASHINGTON DAMSEL NYMPH

Hook: Mustad 9672 or equivalent ~ Size 8, 10, and 12
Tail: Olive marabou
Body: Olive wool yarn
Legs: Pheasant tail fibers
Wing Case: Olive elk hair or turkey tail
Thorax: Olive rabbit fur dubbing
Eyes: *(optional)* 1/4" of Monofilament melted on both ends

GOLD RIBBED HAIR'S EAR
(Impressionistic Nymph, Pupa, or Scud)

Hook: Mustad 9671 ~ Size 8, 10, 12, 14, and 16
Tail: Natural wood duck flank
Rib: Fine gold tinsel
Body: Dubbing from a hare's mask (natural, brown, or olive)
Legs: Whisp of wood duck or mallard fibers
Wing Case: Dyed brown or mottled turkey

TROUT CANDY
(Soft Hackle Kokanee Fly)

Hook: Traditional wet fly or a curved "scud" hook #12 and 14
Body: Wound pearl mylar or flashabou over a thread base
Thorax: Collar of fine ostrich herl
Hackle: Soft gray partridge or dun hen

CONSERVATION

WAYS TO BRING ABOUT POSITIVE CHANGE

Most people interested in outdoor sports, especially fishing, are aware of the negative effect that population growth and development have on the environment. Since we all live, consume, pollute and dwell in this environment, it is nearly impossible for any individual to completely avoid contributing to the problem. The challenge is to have a minimal impact on the environment and our natural resources. In addition to reducing activities that directly harm these resources, it is necessary to conserve them. Well publicized conservation methods include car pooling, recycling, composting, organic gardening and bicycling. With respect to fish and other aquatic life, conservation action can take the form of stream improvement, "no kill" fishing where applicable, packing-out litter, protecting stream or shoreline trees and vegetation, as well as supporting environmental groups that participate in the political process.

The Washington Department of Fish and Wildlife has stated their management goal ... "is to provide for healthy and abundant populations of game fish and allow for a full range of recreational opportunities for all citizens. The challenge ... is to identify ways in which to promote game fish recreation where it has the most public benefit and the least negative impact on the resource". In my opinion, the state has a tough challenge. The WDFW has to sort out all the special recreational interests, then balance the public benefit against the pressure it will put on the resource.

Consider the following paragraph, taken from Data on Selected Lakes in Washington - U.S. Dept. of Interior, Geological Survey 1973 (open file report) ... "Man's use of the lakes in western Washington has grown rapidly, especially within the last 10 years. Lakes are undergoing continual physical, chemical, and biological changes in response to natural or cultural impositions. Unlimited use by man entails increased nutrient enrichment which in turn, accelerates lake eutrophication. It is difficult to predict how recreational development and other uses of the lakes will affect various components of each lake's ecology. Certainly, some aspects of the lakes' environments will be altered. The degree of alteration will depend largely on the implementation of policies setting standards for allowable changes and rates of change".

It has been over 20 years since the foregoing study was undertaken to estimate the effects of population impact on Washington lakes. It is clear that the Dept. of Fish and Wildlife has "implemented policies" to limit the degree of ecological change that can be allowed to take place on our lakes. Through special regulations, slot limits and closed seasons on certain fish species, this is being achieved.

A good example of how special regulations can help protect the chain of aquatic life, is that of Chopaka Lake. In order to protect mayfly populations harmed by oil in the surface film, a restriction was imposed against motors. This resulted in an improved habitat for the trout and has in turn, benefited anglers with better fishing. Of course, one recreational use was lost; the right to run an outboard motor boat - but this is at most a mild inconvenience. Without question, the benefit to the resource far outweighs the inconvenience. Besides, look at all the exercise the fishermen gain by rowing or paddling!

We, as fishing enthusiasts can help create positive change by providing input to state agencies, participating in fishing clubs and their ancillary projects, and by having a general awareness of the environmental problems faced by governments, industry, and the general public. Only through legitimate consultation and cooperation will these problems be solved.

WHATCOM COUNTY

GAME AND

FISH LAWS

✠   ✠

J. M. AITKEN

County Game Warden

Phone Ferndale 410

✠   ✠

1913--1914

S. B. IRISH CO., ━━━━ PRINTING, BELLINGHAM

purpose whatever except as hereinafter provided, any of the game fish hereinafter mentioned within the periods mentioned, to-wit: Any variety of trout except Dolly Varden or bull trout or any variety of pike, between the 31st day of December and the 1st day of May following or any black, grey or Oseego bass cropie, perch, bullhead, or sunfish between the first day of May and the 15th day of July of the same year. Any person violating the provisions of this section shall be guilty of a misdemeanor.

Sec. 42.   Limit of Catch.

No person shall catch, take, kill or have in his possession more than fifty game fish in any one day, nor more than twenty pounds and one game fish in any one day, nor more than thirty pounds and one game fish in any one calendar week, nor in any other manner than by angling for them with hook and line held in the hand or attached to a rod so held, and no person shall have in his possession any game fish caught, taken or killed in any of the waters of this State except as provided in this chapter. Any person violating this section shall be guilty of a misdemeanor.

Sec. 44.   Size of Trout.

No person shall at any time catch, take, kill, or have in his possession or under his control any trout or bass of any variety whatever which are less than six inches in length. Any person catching such game fish shall at once return the same to the water from whence they are taken with as little injury as possible. Any person violating the provisions of this section shall be guilty of a misdemeanor.

Sec. 47.   Fish Ways and Dams.

No person shall catch, take or kill in any stream within four hundred feet of any fish way or dam or have in his possession or under his control any game fish so caught, taken or killed. Any person who violates any of the provisions of this section shall be guilty of a misdemeanor.

Always check the current regulations for special size and catch limits, as well as gear restrictions. Times have changed since the 1913 Game and Fish Laws, pictured above, were administered under county jurisdiction (notice the 50 fish per day possession limit - all species included!) Today, population growth and environmental concerns mandate a more complex, statewide fish management plan.

BIBLIOGRAPHY

Collings, M.R. Data on Selected Lakes in Washington. U.S. Dept. of the Interior, geological survey (1973) open file report. In cooperation with the State of Washington Dept. of Ecology.

Jackson, S. and Lovgren, T. Field Performance Evaluation of Three Rainbow Trout Broodstocks In Western Washington Lowland Lakes, (October 1992). Washington Department of Wildlife - Fisheries Management Division, Progress Report No: 92-19.

Kerwin, John E. Annual Report Hatcheries and Semi-Natural Rearing Ponds. (June 1991) Washington Dept. of Wildlife.

Washington Department of Wildlife. Final Recommendations Washington Game Fish Seasons, Catch Limits, and Regulations 1992-1994; Fisheries Management Division.

Wolcott, Ernest E. Lakes of Washington; Department of Conservation, Division of Water Resources - Water Supply Bulletin (1964). Volumes I and II (eastern and western Wa.).

Miscellaneous government pamphlets and bulletins published for distribution to the public, including stocking reports and prospects, Trout of Washington, and the game fish regulations.

ABOUT THE AUTHOR

Dan Homel has fished extensively for all species of trout throughout the State of Washington and in many other areas of the Northwest. As a former fly fishing shop owner and fly tying instructor he has advised numerous beginners on the art of fishing with a fly. Dan was a founder of the conservation group Washington Trout, and is a past vice-president of the Fourth Corner Fly Fishers. He is a member of the Northwest Outdoor Writers Association.

Ask your local bookseller for Dan's other titles:

Diary of Northwest Trout Flies - 96 pages. Detailed patterns are presented for 35 productive Pacific Northwest trout flies. These are local favorites, old reliables, and a few of the author and illustrator's own designs. Each fly was drawn, in pen and ink, by wildlife artist Ed Ruckey. Tying and fishing notes are included, along with 3 special Ralph Wahl photographs! (Forrest-Park Publishers $7.95) ISBN: 1-879522-00-4.

Old Fishing Tackle and Collectibles - 96 pages. A history, identification, and value guide to bamboo rods, antique reels, wood and metal lures, fly fishing collectibles, ephemera and more! Laminated four-color cover with numerous black and white photographs. (Forrest-Park Publishers $10.95) ISBN: 1-879522-02-0

Collector's Guide to Old Fishing Reels - 96 pages. A complete guide dedicated specifically to collectible and antique reels. Fly, Spin, casting, big game and wood reels are included with 50 detailed B&W photographs. (Forrest-Park Publishers $9.95) ISBN: 1-879522-01-2

Good resident trout streams are rare in the Pacific Northwest, so anglers keep them a secret! Veteran Washington fly fisher, Richard VanDemark, is seen here wading at a spot known only as "the quiet pool."